▶▶ FastForward™

with Rikky Rooksby

A progressive approach to chords you can learn today!

Acoustic Guitar Chords

Wise Publications
London / New York / Sydney / Paris / Copenhagen / Madrid

Exclusive Distributors:
Music Sales Limited
8/9 Frith Street, London W1V 5TZ, England.
Music Sales Pty Limited
120 Rothschild Avenue, Rosebery, NSW 2018, Australia.
Music Sales Corporation
257 Park Avenue South, New York, NY10010,
United States of America.

Order No.AM950940
ISBN 0-7119-7065-3
This book © Copyright 1998 by Wise Publications.

Unauthorised reproduction of any part of this
publication by any means including photocopying is
an infringement of copyright.

Book design by Michael Bell Design.
Edited and arranged by Rikky Rooksby.
Music processed by Barnes Music Engraving
Cover photography by George Taylor
Cover instrument kindly loaned by World Of Music

Text photographs courtesy of London Features
International

Printed in the United Kingdom by Page Bros.,
Norwich, Norfolk..

Your Guarantee of Quality:
As publishers, we strive to produce every book to
the highest commercial standards.
The music has been freshly engraved and the book has
been carefully designed to minimise awkward page turns
and to make playing from it a real pleasure.
Particular care has been given to specifying acid-free,
neutral-sized paper made from pulps which have not
been elemental chlorine bleached.
This pulp is from farmed sustainable forests and
was produced with special regard for the environment.
Throughout, the printing and binding have
been planned to ensure a sturdy, attractive publication
which should give years of enjoyment.
If your copy fails to meet our high standards, please
inform us and we will gladly replace it.

Music Sales' complete catalogue describes
thousands of titles and is available in full colour sections
by subject, direct from Music Sales Limited.
Please state your areas of interest and send a cheque/postal
order for £1.50 for postage to: Music Sales Limited,
Newmarket Road, Bury St. Edmunds, Suffolk IP33 3YB.

Visit the Internet Music Shop at
http://www.musicsales.co.uk

Introduction
Learning Chords 4

Basic Chord Shapes
1. Getting Started 6
Twelve Easy Chords 6
2. Major Chords 13
3. Minor Chords 17
4. Combining Major And Minor 20
5. Flats And Sharps 24

Strumming Patterns And Barre Chords
6. Strumming Patterns 27
7. The Barre Chord 31
8. Changing An Open Chord Into A Barre Chord 31
9. Playing The Same Chord In Different Positions 37

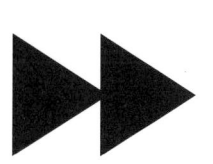

Taking Chords Further
10. Woke Up This Mornin' – The Dominant Seventh 38
11. This Chord's In Love – The Major Seventh 44
12. It's Getting Better – The Minor Seventh 48
13. A Jagged Edge – The Suspended Fourth 52
14. Tension On The Highwire – The Suspended Second 54
15. Just Fab – Major Sixths 57

Putting It All Together
16. Complete Song – Tuesday's Queen 60

Congratulations 63

Introduction

Hello, and welcome to ▶▶Fast*Forward*

Congratulations on purchasing a product that will improve your playing and provide you with hours of pleasure. All the music in this book has been specially created by professional musicians to give you maximum value and enjoyment.

If you already know how to 'drive' your instrument, but you'd like to do a little customising, you've pulled in at the right place. We'll put you on the fast track to playing the riffs and patterns that today's professionals rely on.

We'll provide you with a vocabulary of riffs that you can apply in a wide variety of musical situations, with a special emphasis on giving you the techniques that will help you in a band situation.

That's why the music examples in this book come with full-band audio tracks so that you get your chance to join in. All players and bands get their sounds and styles by drawing on the same basic building blocks. With ▶▶Fast*Forward* you'll learn these quickly, and then be ready to use them to create your own style.

Learning Chords

With just a little technique you can create a great sound, by simply strumming chords on your guitar. In fact, there are many professional guitarists and singers whose technique doesn't go much beyond just this. Of course, this is part of the guitar's popularity – most people can learn to strum chords (and unlike the piano, the guitar is eminently portable).

Maybe you've seen people busking on the streets, or singing songs at parties and thought you'd like to do the same. You just need to know some shapes and be able to change quickly enough from one chord to the next. This book will show you how. If you can't read music, don't worry – there isn't any!

Many books give you pages and pages of chord shapes. ▶▶Fast*Forward* *Acoustic Guitar Chords* is different. As you work through the book, you'll learn not only the shapes but also how groups of chords differ from one another, and the various musical situations in which they might be used. It's a progressive method.

You'll start with some shapes which are easy to play, so you'll be getting great sounds from your guitar straight away! Then you'll be introduced step-by-step to the chords that are most commonly used in folk, pop and rock songs. Finally, you'll have the opportunity to play your way through a whole song.

This book can be used by any guitarist, whether you have a nylon-strung 'Classical' (or 'Spanish') guitar, a steel-strung acoustic (or 'folk' guitar), or even a 12-string, a semi-acoustic or a solid-body electric. If you want to play chords finger-style use this book in conjunction with the ▶▶**FastForward** *Finger-Picking Guitar* book.

Each musical example is played once with the rhythm guitar part, and once without. The first track is for you to learn by listening, the second track is for you to practise along with. The second track has a guitar chord on the first beat of each bar to give you a helping hand. The early examples are set to a slow tempo to give you a chance to change between chords smoothly. As the book goes on you'll find that the tempos will gradually increase.

The examples have a one-bar count-in.

Basic Chord Shapes

1. Getting Started

Make sure you are holding the guitar comfortably.

If you are right-handed, the guitar should be resting on your right thigh. Let your right arm rest on the top of the guitar in a relaxed way – it should rest diagonally across the instrument so that your hand is near the soundhole. Make sure that the guitar neck is not pointing below the horizontal (i.e. towards the floor) – if anything, it should be pointing slightly upwards. This makes certain chords easier to play.

Your left thumb should be placed on the neck, somewhere behind the first and second fingers. The thumb position changes depending on the chord shape, as you will see.

Although it is possible to strum chords using either the right-hand thumb or the fingers, I recommend you use a pick or plectrum.

A pick gives a more even sound and, when you need it, more volume. The pick is held between the thumb and first finger – don't use the second finger, because there are certain guitar styles you may want to use later, that involve playing with a pick and fingers. Don't hold the pick too rigidly, and make sure that you keep your hand relaxed.

The pick should be of a light kind, that is to say, sufficiently thin that you can easily bend it. Light picks give a much better tone than hard ones, which sound 'lumpy' – especially on acoustics. You will hear a slight 'click' each time the pick hits the strings – this is normal, and adds a pleasing element of percussion to the chords.

Twelve Easy Chords

Now it's time to look at your first chords. These are drawn in chord boxes. Each box shows the strings running vertically, and the frets running horizontally. The string on the extreme left of the box is the lowest-pitched E string; the string on the extreme right is the highest-pitched E string.

The circled numbers indicate left-hand fingers holding down the strings. An 'x' above a string means don't play it. An 'o' means this is an open (unfretted) string which you can play.

Underneath the chord box you'll see a row of letters and a row of numbers. The letters tell you the exact notes you're playing, and the numbers indicate whereabouts in the scale those notes occur.

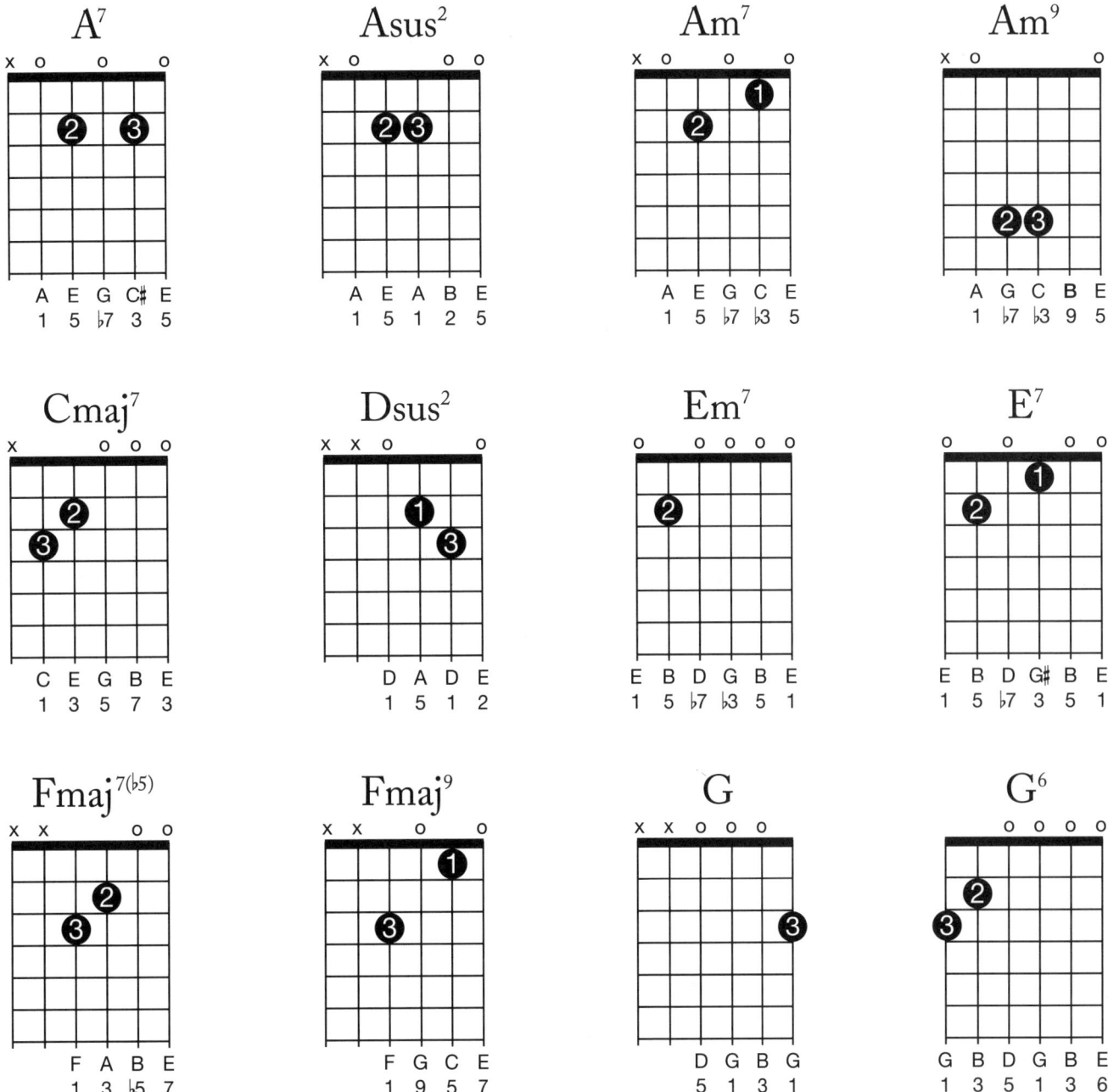

These chords have been chosen purely because they are easy to play. As you try them out, check each string to make sure it rings without interference from another finger on an adjacent string, which might be touching it.

Place your fretting fingers close to the metal frets, but don't actually touch them. If you touch the fret the note will be dulled; if you are too far away the string will buzz.

Now let your fretting hand touch all the strings, anywhere on the neck, so none of them can ring, and try strumming gently up and down. All you'll hear will be a dull, clicking tone, but you'll be able to get accustomed to the physical action. Most of the movement for strumming should come from the forearm.

PETER BUCK (REM)
"I like rhythm guitar; I don't like too much fiddling around; I don't really need to show off in the context of the band."

Exercise 1

Hold down the A7 chord and strum up and down for eight bars. The :|| sign at the end of this example simply means return to the beginning and play the sequence again.

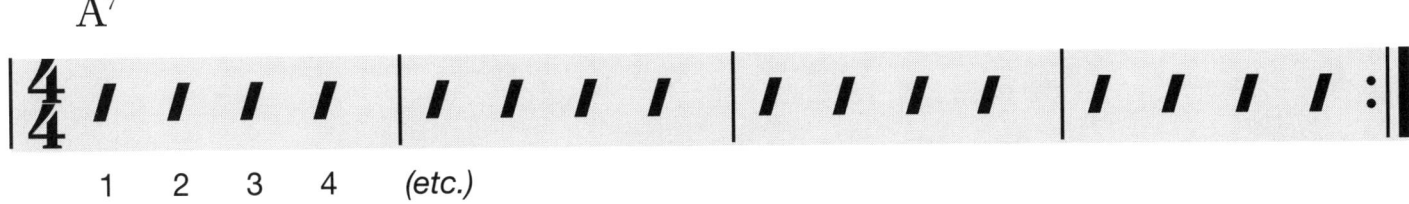

Exercise 2

Now practise a change from Cmaj7 to Am7. You'll see that this only requires you to lift up your 3rd finger and put your 1st finger down. The 2nd finger doesn't move.

Exercise 3

To go from Em7 to E7 just put your 1st finger down. The E7 shape is then moved across the fretboard by one string to get Am7. Add the 3rd finger to get Fmaj9 and you're there!

▶▶ THE EDGE
"When I'm working on a song or a guitar part, the subconscious kicks in and it proves itself far more capable of giving you the answer than the conscious mind."

Exercise 4

Notice that G6 and Cmaj7 are the same shape but on different strings. Move the Asus2 shape up three frets, and it becomes Am9!

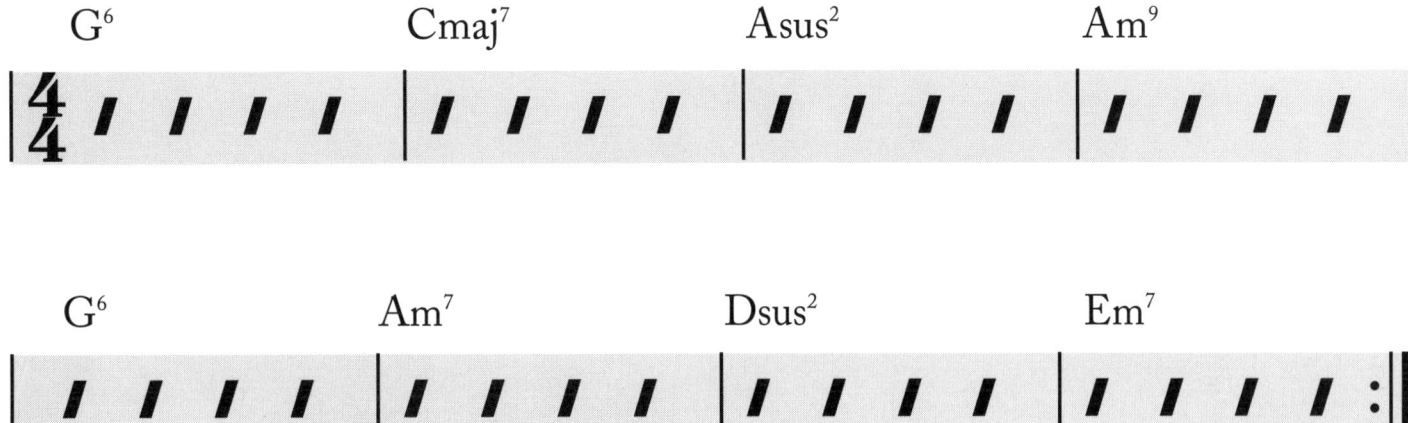

If you're playing the guitar for the first time your fingers may get sore. Guitarists develop hard pads of skin on their fretting fingers after a few weeks of practice.

If you can't keep up with the backing track at first, don't worry – set your own slower tempo by tapping your foot steadily and playing to that rhythm.

You will need to learn the shapes before you can change chords in tempo. Your fingers have to know exactly where they're going to stand a chance of getting there in time with the beat.

▶ **PAUL WELLER**
"If a song still sounds good when you sit down and play it with just a voice and a guitar then you know you've got a good song."

2. Major Chords

Here's the first proper category of chords, the majors. These are the most important chords – they sound happy and cheerful.

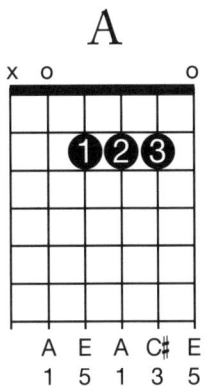
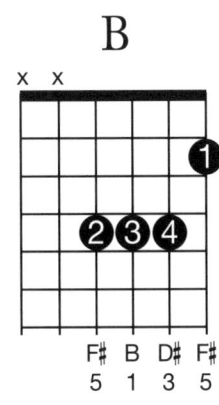
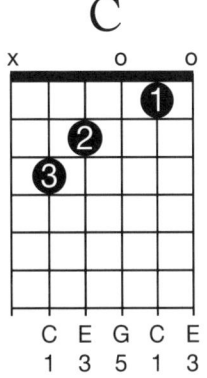
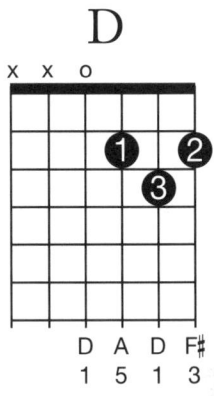

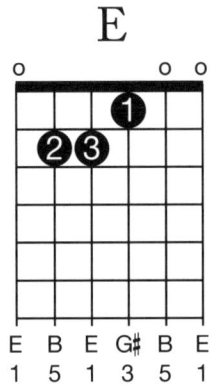
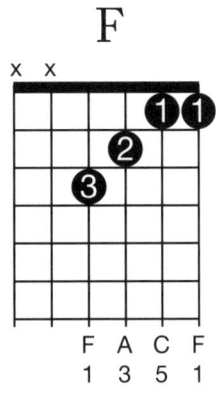
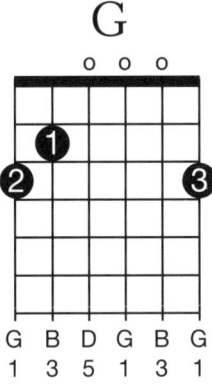

You may find B major slightly awkward at first because of the stretch from fret 2 to fret 4. Similarly, F major may be tricky because it requires the first finger to hold down the top two strings. This is called a 'half-barre'.

To play the half-barre, put your first finger onto the strings and squeeze by pulling slightly toward the nut (the piece of plastic or metal with notches in, which guides the strings toward the machineheads). As the string tension is very great at this point on the fretboard, you may find it helpful to move the chord shape up a few frets – try it at the 3rd or 4th fret where the string tension is less. Another useful technique for this type of chord is to drop your fretting hand thumb down to the middle of the neck, still pointing upwards.

A, B, C, D, E, F and G are the seven most common major chords for songs. These are the major chords built on root notes which correspond to the white keys on a piano.

Exercise 5

When changing from A to D, notice that your 3rd finger stays on the same string – it just moves up a fret. This is called a 'guide finger'. Watch out for guide fingers throughout this book – they make chord changing much easier. When you change from D to E, the guide finger is the 1st finger.

Exercise 6

Watch out for the B chord!

Exercise 7

When changing from C to G you may find it easier to play the G chord with your 2nd, 3rd and 4th fingers.

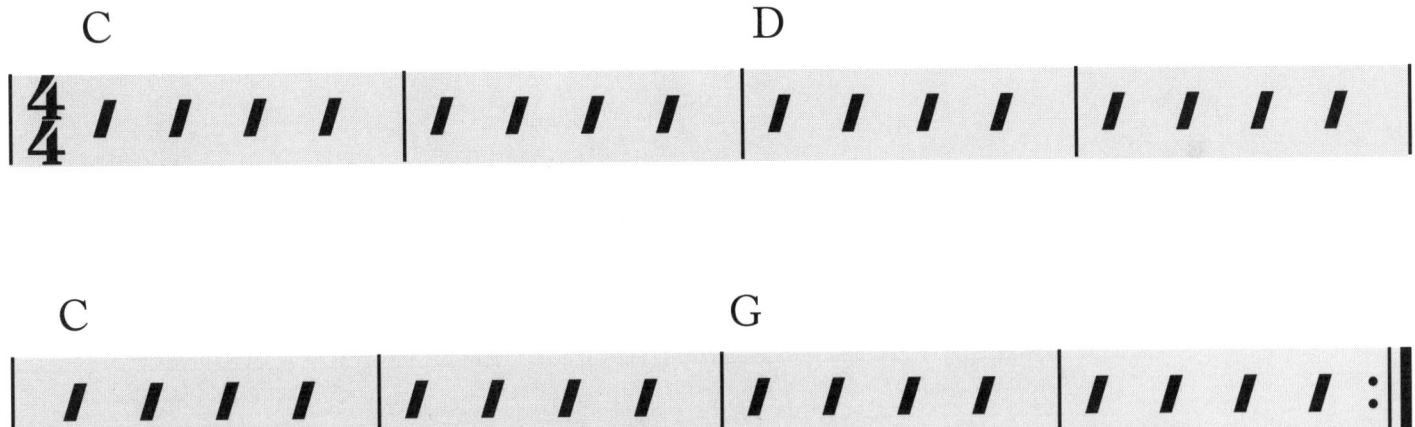

Exercise 8

Here's your chance to practise F. When you move to C, release the half-barre and let your 1st finger rise so that it can hold down the 2nd string. If you find the F too difficult, substitute the Fmaj9 from the 12 easy chords section.

▶▶ **NEIL YOUNG**

"I try not to think about the songs that I write, I just try to write them. And I try not to edit them ... I know there's a source where music comes through you."

3. Minor Chords

The minor chords are almost as important as the major chords. By comparison with the majors, they sound sad.

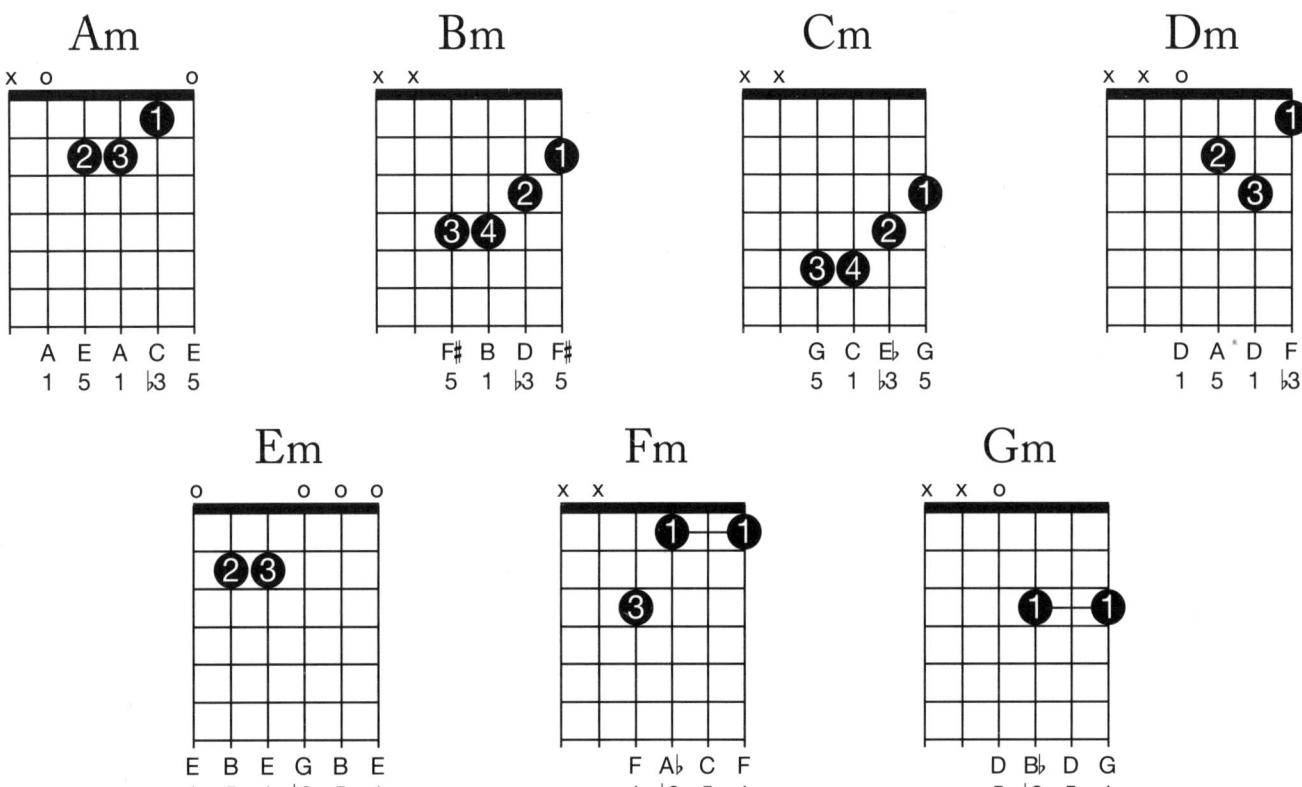

Am, Dm and Em are the easiest. The hardest is Fm, which requires a half-barre over three strings. Use the 'squeeze' technique described in the previous section, and try this chord shape higher up the neck, at the 3rd or 4th fret. The Gm chord is a also a half-barre, but an easier one, since it doesn't require any other fingers.

Exercise 9

Notice how the second and third fingers used for Em are moved across a string to form the basis for Am.

TRACKS 18+19

| Em | Am | Em | Am |

17

▶▶ **KEITH RICHARDS**
"I didn't say I was a rhythm guitarist, other people made my reputation for me."

Exercise 10

When changing from Dm to Bm use your
1st finger on the 1st string as a guide.

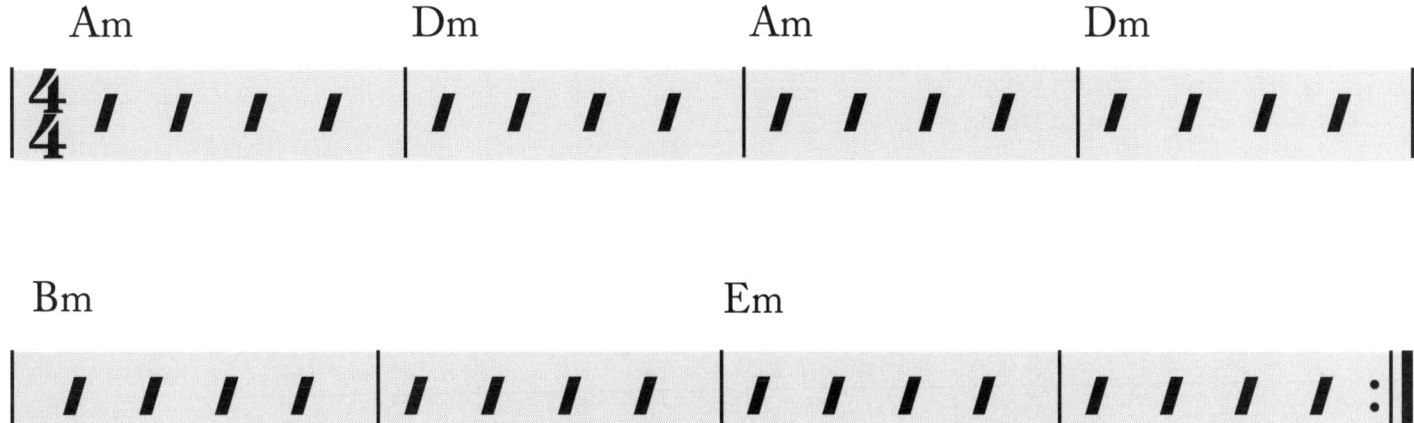

Exercise 11

No guide fingers on this one!

4. Combining Major And Minor

Most songs combine major and minor chords in their sequences. Music fluctuates from the sadness of the minors to the happiness of the majors and back again.

You can now try some chord progressions which mix major and minor chords. If some of these sequences remind you of famous songs, don't be surprised. They are progressions which have been climbing the charts over and over again in the past 40 years.

Exercise 12

To move from C to Am you only need to move one finger. When changing from F to Dm notice that your 2nd finger doesn't move.

TRACKS 24+25

C	Am	C	Am
4/4 / / / /	/ / / /	/ / / /	/ / / /

F	Dm	F	Dm
/ / / /	/ / / /	/ / / /	/ / / / :||

20 ▶▶FastForward Acoustic Guitar Chords

Exercise 13

Watch out for the half-barre Gm in the last bar of this exercise!

TRACKS 26+27

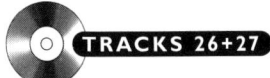

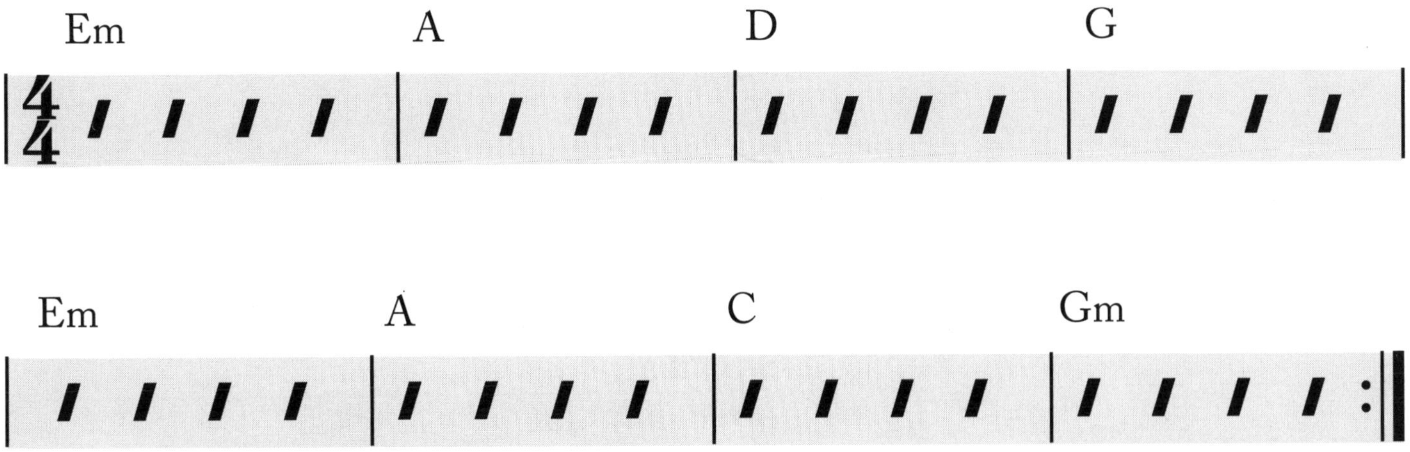
Em
A
D
G
Em
A
C
Gm

Exercise 14

You should recognise some of these changes!

TRACKS 28+29

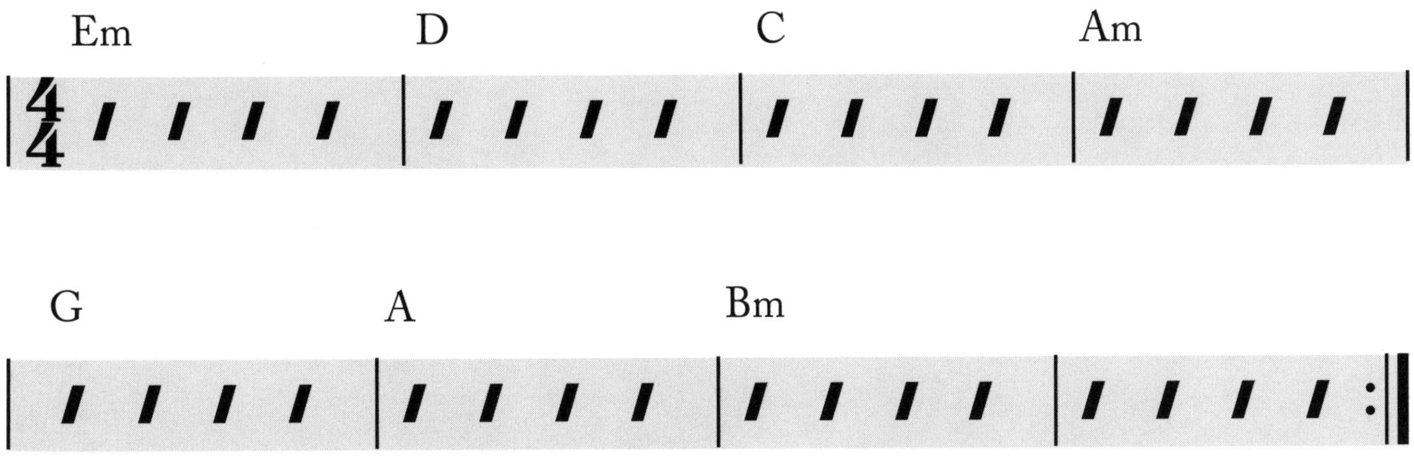
Em
D
C
Am
G
A
Bm

▶▶ *ERIC CLAPTON*
"When I was 14 or 15 they gave me a real guitar, an acoustic, but it was hard to play. But I did invent chords. I invented E and I invented A. I thought I had discovered something incredible."

Exercise 15

This is fairly straightforward, apart from the F major chord in the last bar.

D	Em	G	A
4/4 / / / /	/ / / /	/ / / /	/ / / /

D	C	Em	F
/ / / /	/ / / /	/ / / /	/ / / / :||

5. Flats And Sharps

Music uses 12 notes: A, B, C, D, E, F, and G, and the five in-between notes which have two names each: A♯/B♭, C♯/D♭, D♯/E♭, F♯/G♭, and G♯/A♭. These are the black keys on the piano.

The flat/sharp major and minor chords are not as easy to play as the other chords you've encountered so far. As a result they are not used as frequently by guitarists. We're not going to use any of these in our example tracks, but you should know where to find them if you need them. The shapes given are the easiest, but not the only, way of playing these chords.

Major Sharp/Flat Chords

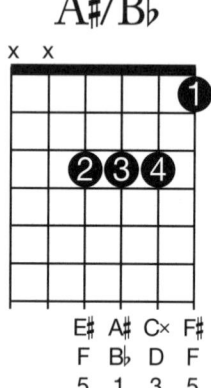
A♯/B♭

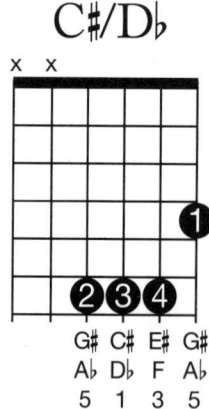
C♯/D♭

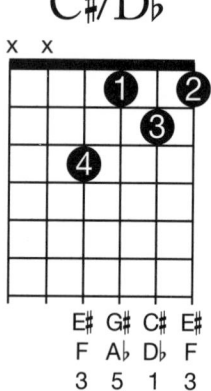
C♯/D♭

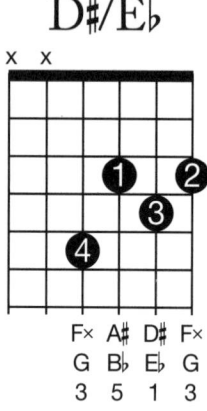
D♯/E♭

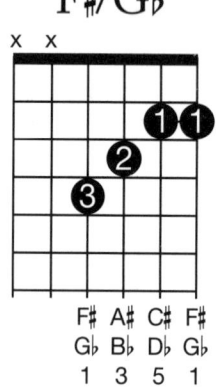
F♯/G♭

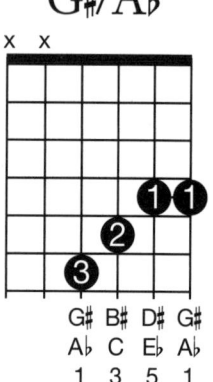
G♯/A♭

Minor Sharp/Flat Chords

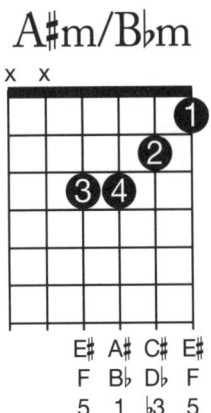
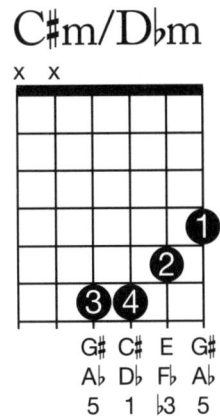
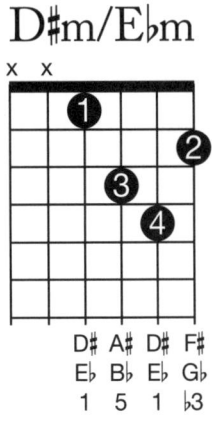
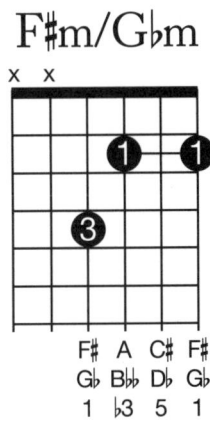
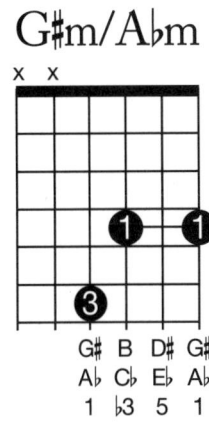

25

▶▶ **BRUCE SPRINGSTEEN**
"When I started I just wanted to play rhythm guitar. Just stand back and play rhythm, no singing or anything."

Strumming Patterns And Barre Chords
6. Strumming Patterns

Now that you've learnt some chords, let's pause for a second and think about what your right hand is doing. The next exercises will give you ideas for strumming patterns – all your left hand needs to do is hold down an A chord.

Exercise 16

This is a progressive exercise in which you gradually hit the A chord more frequently.

By the final bars you will be strumming 8th notes, two to each beat.

 TRACKS 32+33

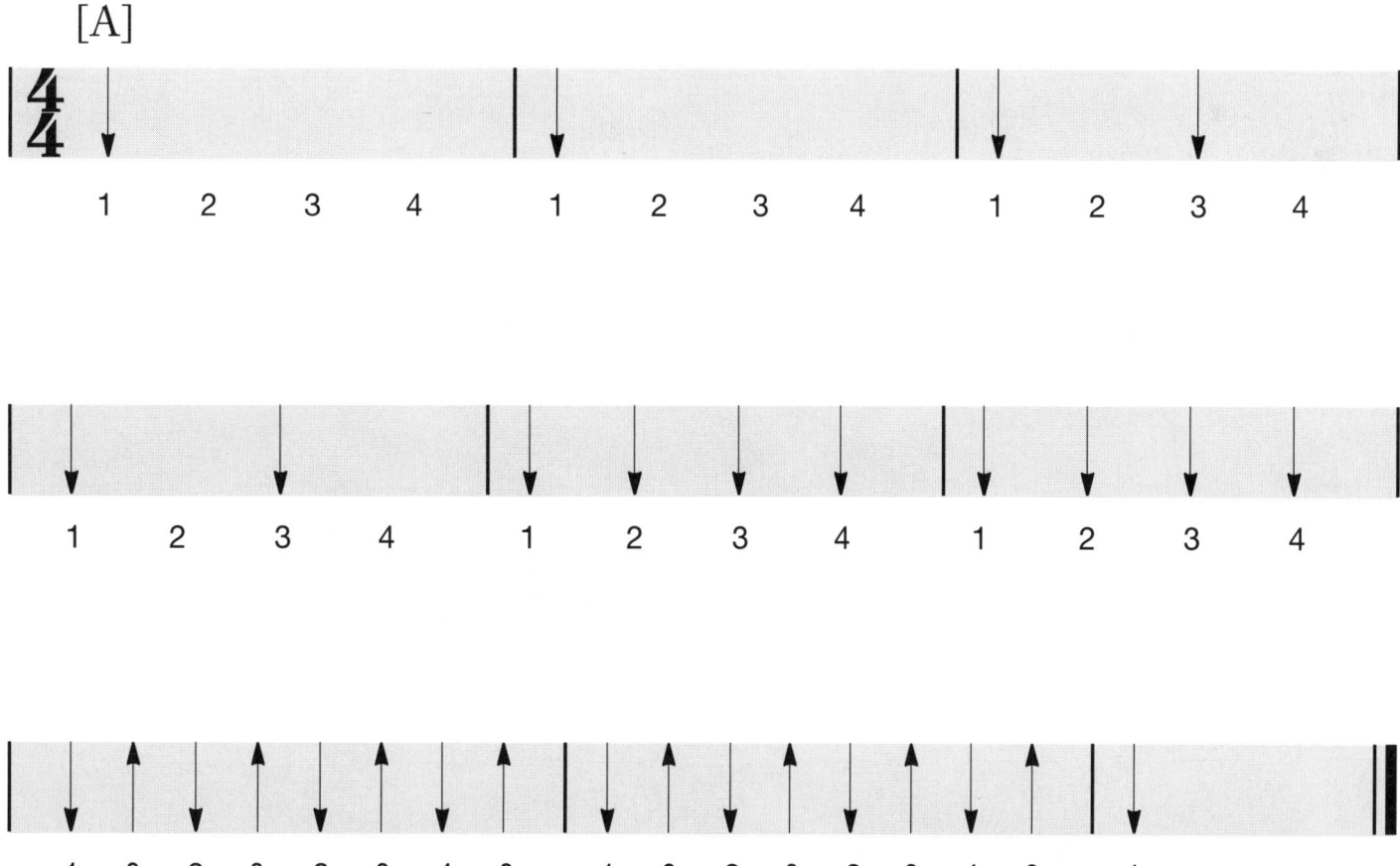

▶▶ *NOEL GALLAGHER*
"Bonehead will put down a rhythm track and I'll put down a rhythm track. He's not allowed to play open chords: he plays barre chords and then I'll put down a rhythm track of just open chords."

Exercise 17

Now let's do the reverse: start strumming 8ths and gradually reduce the number of times you hit the chord in a bar.

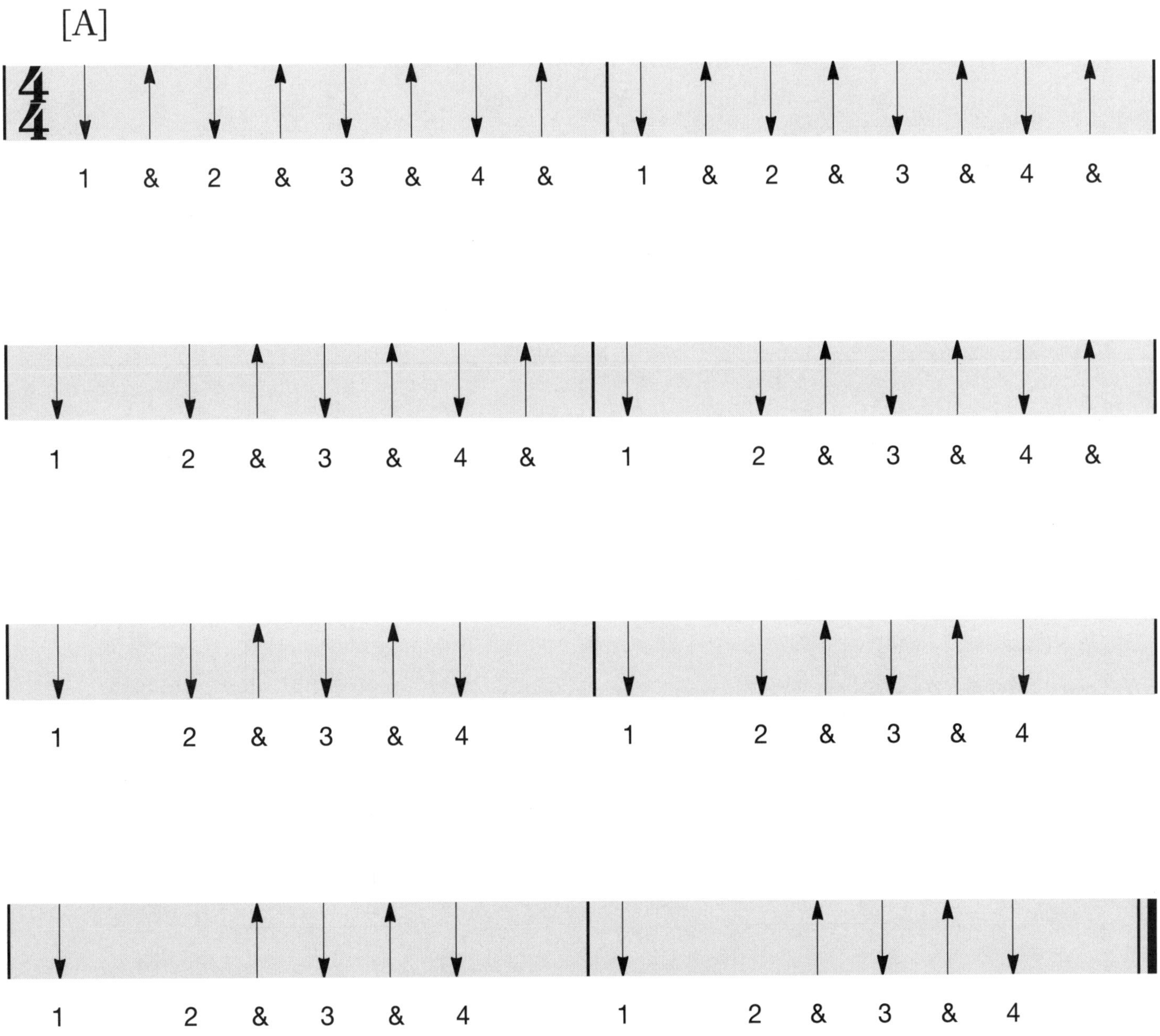

Exercise 18

You don't always have to play on every down-beat. This example involves resting on some of the beats, and instead strumming on off-beats. This gives a distinctive 'syncopated' feel.

[A]

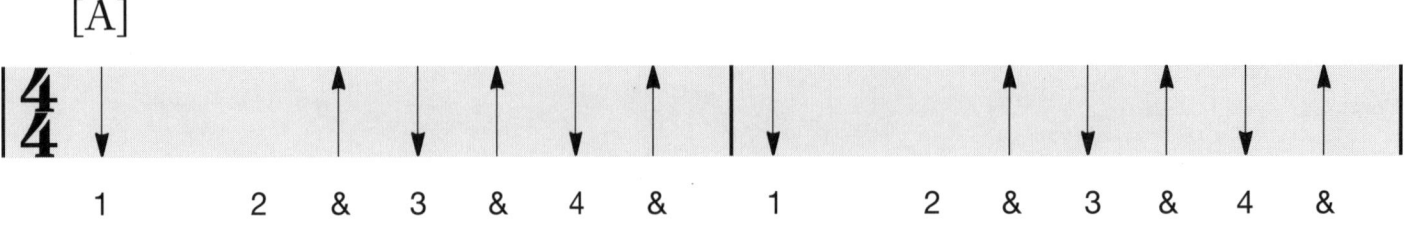

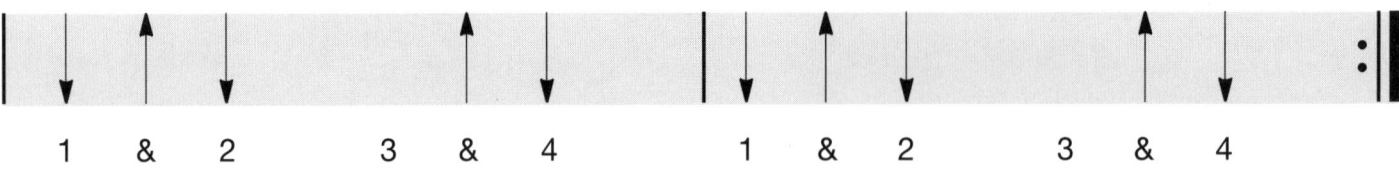

It's vital to keep a steady rhythm going; however, because the guitar sustains notes once they have been struck, a chord will resonate if you hold it – this means you don't *have* to keep striking the chord. You can allow it to ring across some beats. Most strumming you'll hear on records does this – allowing the chords to ring over the beat prevents monotony.

On the remaining musical examples you'll be strumming down on the first beat, and then down and up on the other three beats. However, feel free to experiment with different strumming patterns over the backing tracks.

7. The Barre Chord

Most of the chords you have practised so far have been 'open string' chords. That is, they contain one or more open (unfretted) strings. They are easy to play and ring nicely on the guitar. You have also played chords like F, Fm, and Gm, which needed one finger to hold down more than one string – the half-barre.

We're now ready to move on to the 'full barre', which involves a finger (usually the 1st) stretching over four, five, or even six strings.

This type of chord has been deliberately omitted from most of the exercises because it needs a lot of practice. However, to get the most out of your guitar, you'll need to know how an open string chord can be changed into an barre chord.

How hard a barre chord is to play partly depends on your guitar. Light-gauge strings can help – the strings need to be close to the fretboard (what is called a 'low action'). Keep your fretting hand thumb low behind the neck.

8. Changing An Open Chord Into A Barre Chord

Barre chords are movable. Once you have formed a barre chord it can be moved up the neck and played at any fret.

Look at these transformations, following the chord boxes from left to right.

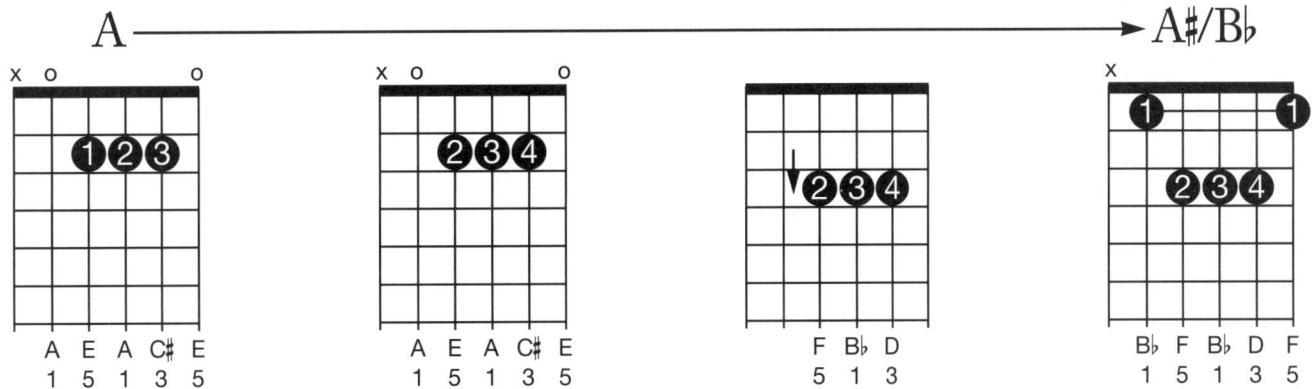

▶▶ **BILLIE JOE (GREEN DAY)**
"I've never been a guitar player's guitar player. I sort of come from the Pete Townshend school - just play rhythm and work inside your own limitations."

▶▶ FastForward™ Guide To Guitar

All You Need To Know to get you started!

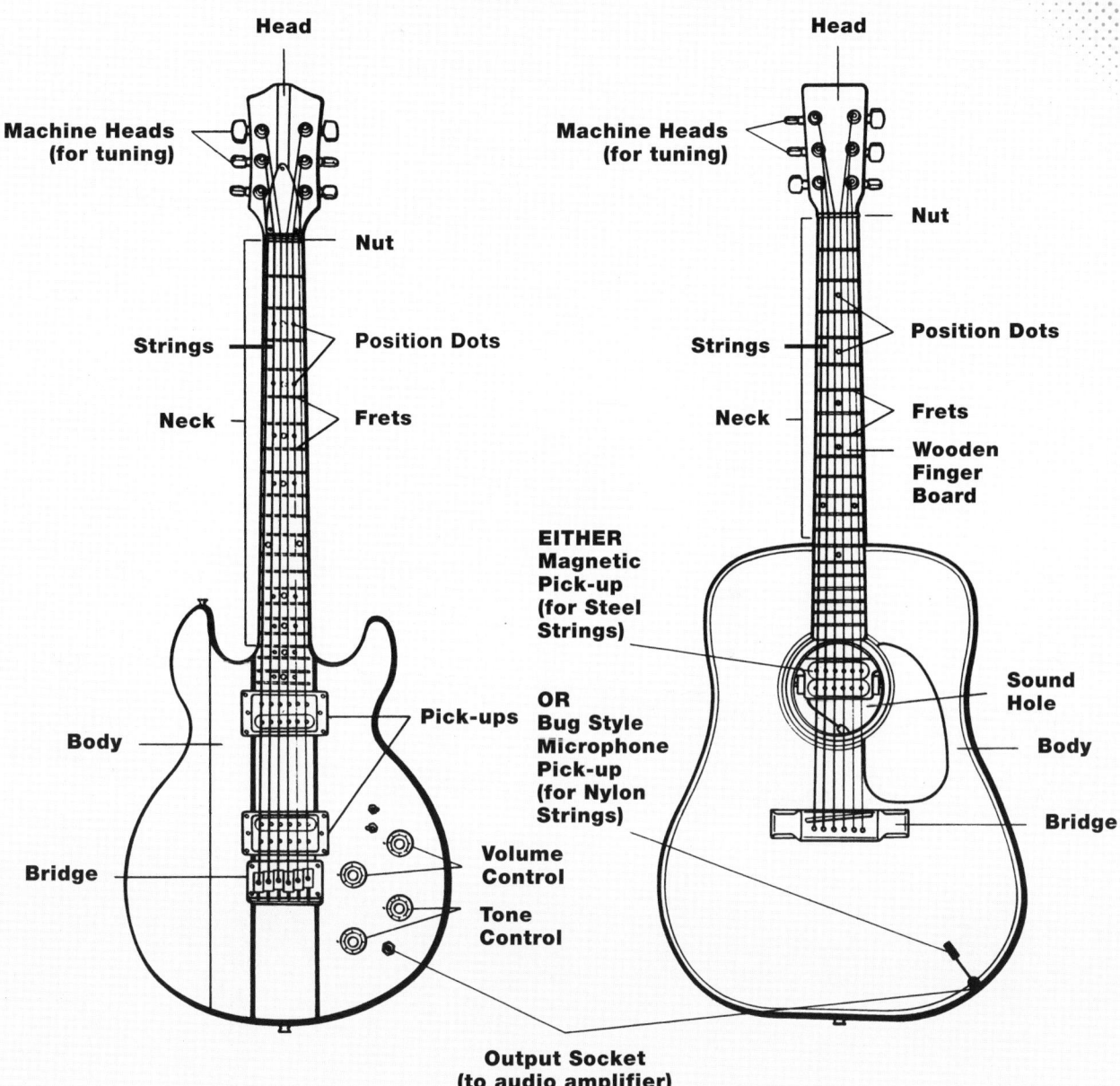

The Guitar

Whether you have an acoustic or an electric guitar, the principles of playing are fundamentally the same, and so are most of the features on both instruments.

In order to 'electrify' an acoustic guitar (as in the diagram), a magnetic pick up can be attached to those guitars with steel strings or a 'bug' style microphone pick-up can be attached to guitars with nylon strings.

If in doubt check with your local music shop.

Pull-Out Chart

Tuning Your Guitar

Tuning
Accurate tuning of the guitar is essential, and is achieved by winding the machine heads up or down. It is always better to 'tune up' to the correct pitch rather than down.

Therefore, if you find that the pitch of your string is higher (sharper) than the correct pitch, you should 'wind down' below the correct pitch, and then 'tune up' to it.

Relative Tuning
Tuning the guitar to itself without the aid of a pitch pipe or other tuning device.

Other Methods Of Tuning
Pitch pipe
Tuning fork
Dedicated electronic guitar tuner

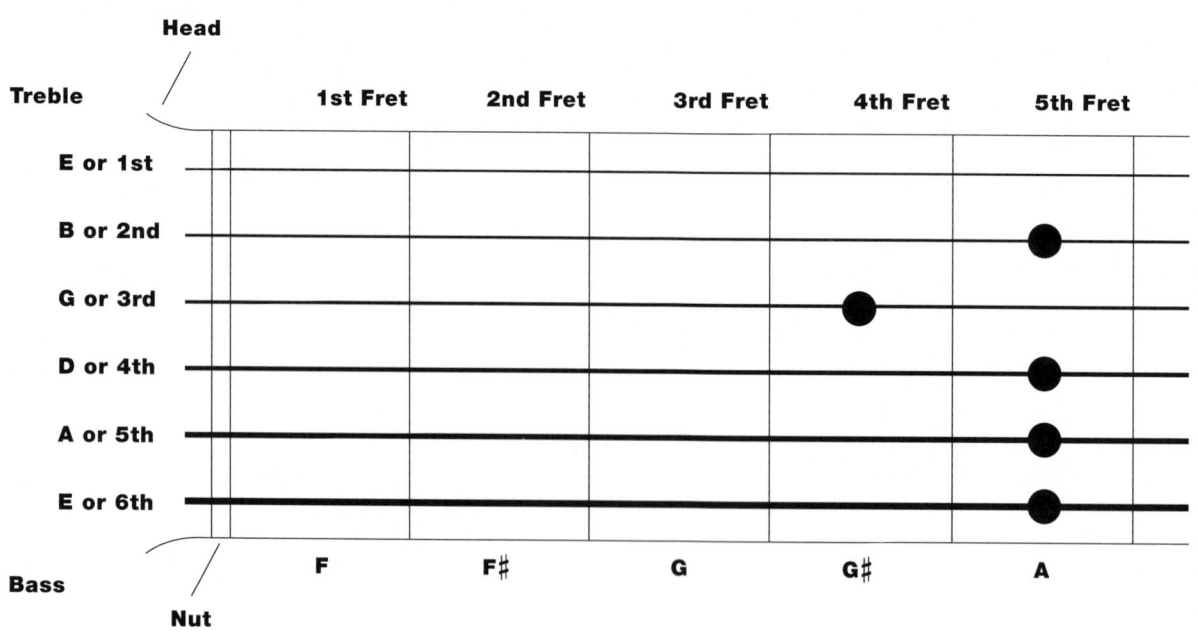

● *Press down where indicated, one at a time, following the instructions below.*

Estimate the pitch of the 6th string as near as possible to **E** or at least a comfortable pitch (not too high or you might break other strings in tuning up).

Then, while checking the various positions on the above diagram, place a finger from your left hand on:

- The 5th fret of the E or 6th string and **tune the open A** (or 5th string) to the note (A)

- The 5th fret of the A or 5th string and **tune the open D** (or 4th string) to the note (D)

- The 5th fret of the D or 4th string and **tune the open G** (or 3rd string) to the note (G)

- The 4th fret of the G or 3rd string and **tune the open B** (or 2nd string) to the note (B)

- The 5th fret of the B or 2nd string and **tune the open E** (or 1st string) to the note (E)

Chord Boxes

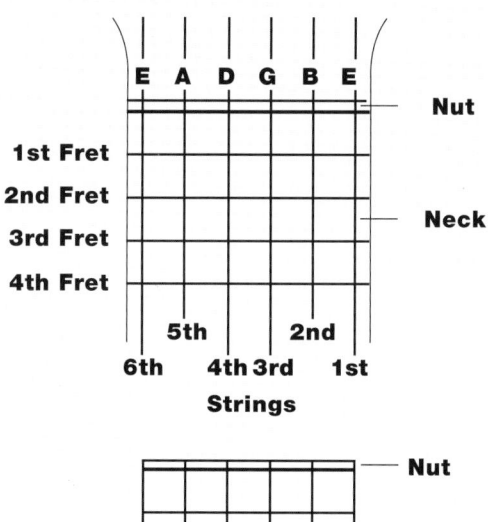

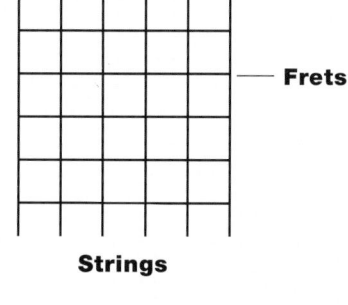

The A Chord

x = do not play this string

All chords are major chords unless otherwise indicated.

Left Hand
Place all three fingers into position and press down firmly. Keep your thumb around the middle of the back of the neck and directly behind your 1st and 2nd fingers.

Right Hand Thumb Or Plectrum
Slowly play each string, starting with the 5th or A string and moving up to the 1st or E string.

If there is any buzzing, perhaps you need to:-
Position your fingers nearer the metal fret (towards you); or adjust the angle of your hand; or check that the buzz is not elsewhere on the guitar by playing the open strings in the same manner.

Finally, your nails may be too long, in which case you are pressing down at an extreme angle and therefore not firmly enough. Also the pad of one of your fingers may be in the way of the next string for the same reason.

So, cut your nails to a more comfortable length and then try to keep them as near vertical to the fretboard as possible.

Once you have a 'buzz-free' sound, play the chord a few times and then remove your fingers and repeat the exercise until your positioning is right instinctively.

Chord boxes are diagrams of the guitar neck viewed head upwards, face on, as illustrated in the above drawings. The horizontal double line at the top is the nut, the other horizontal lines are the frets. The vertical lines are the strings starting from E or 6th on the left to E or 1st on the right.

Any dots with numbers inside them simply indicate which finger goes where. Any strings marked with an **x** must not be played.

The fingers of your hand are numbered 1, 2, 3, & 4 as in the diagram below.

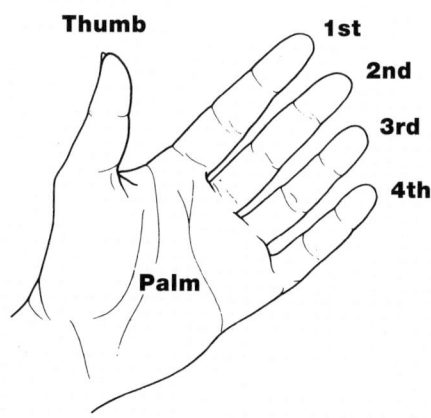

Holding The Guitar

The picture above shows a comfortable position for playing rock or pop guitar

The Right Hand
When STRUMMING (brushing your fingers across the strings), hold your fingers together.

When PICKING (plucking strings individually), hold your wrist further away from the strings than for strumming.

Keep your thumb slightly to the left of your fingers which should be above the three treble strings as shown.

The Plectrum
Many modern guitar players prefer to use a plectrum to strike the strings. Plectrums come in many sizes, shapes and thicknesses and are available from your local music shop.

Start with a fairly large, soft one if possible, with a grip. The photo shows the correct way to hold your plectrum.

The Left Hand
Use your fingertips to press down on the strings in the positions described. Your thumb should be behind your 1st and 2nd fingers pressing on the middle of the back of the neck.

Box 1 is an open A chord. Box 2 shows a different fingering, which will leave your 1st finger free. Now move this shape up one fret (see box 3). Finally, put a barre down with the 1st finger, so that the open strings are all held down at the first fret. Hey presto! An open A chord has become a barre A♯/B♭. If this shape was moved up to the 2nd fret it would become B. At the 3rd fret it would be C – and so on. If you moved it up 12 frets it would become A again – only a much higher-sounding chord.

Transformations for C, D, E, Am, Dm and Em are also given below.

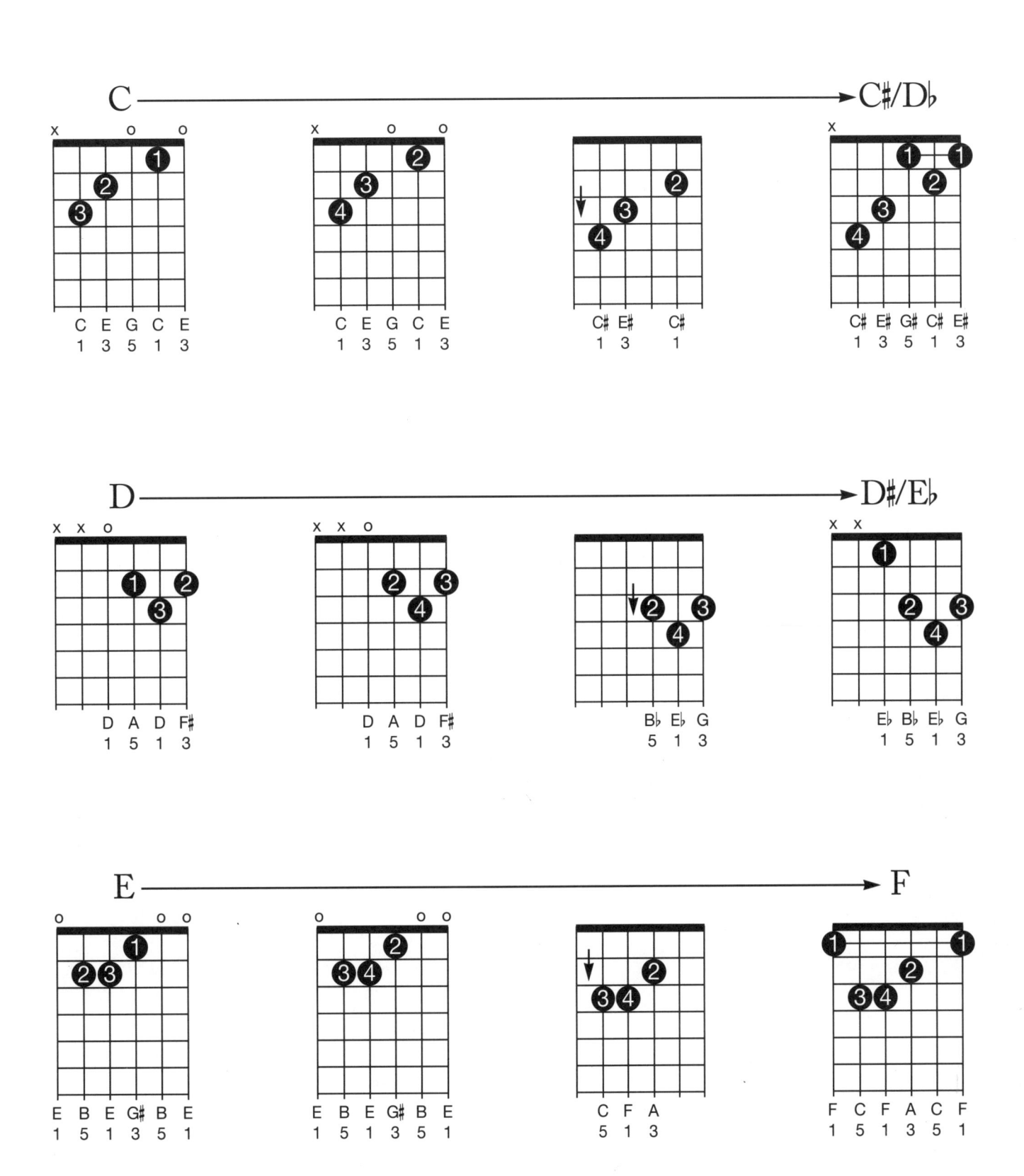

C ⟶ C♯/D♭

| C E G C E | C E G C E | C♯ E♯   C♯ | C♯ E♯ G♯ C♯ E♯ |
| 1 3 5 1 3 | 1 3 5 1 3 | 1 3   1 | 1 3 5 1 3 |

D ⟶ D♯/E♭

| D A D F♯ | D A D F♯ | B♭ E♭ G | E♭ B♭ E♭ G |
| 1 5 1 3 | 1 5 1 3 | 5 1 3 | 1 5 1 3 |

E ⟶ F

| E B E G♯ B E | E B E G♯ B E | C F A | F C F A C F |
| 1 5 1 3 5 1 | 1 5 1 3 5 1 | 5 1 3 | 1 5 1 3 5 1 |

▶▶ RICHARD OAKES (SUEDE)
"I worked out how to play the A chord. About three months afterward, I got heavily into The Clash, and found out that most of their songs revolved around the A chord. I mean, 'White Riot' has only got two chords and I could play them all!"

Am → A#m/B♭m

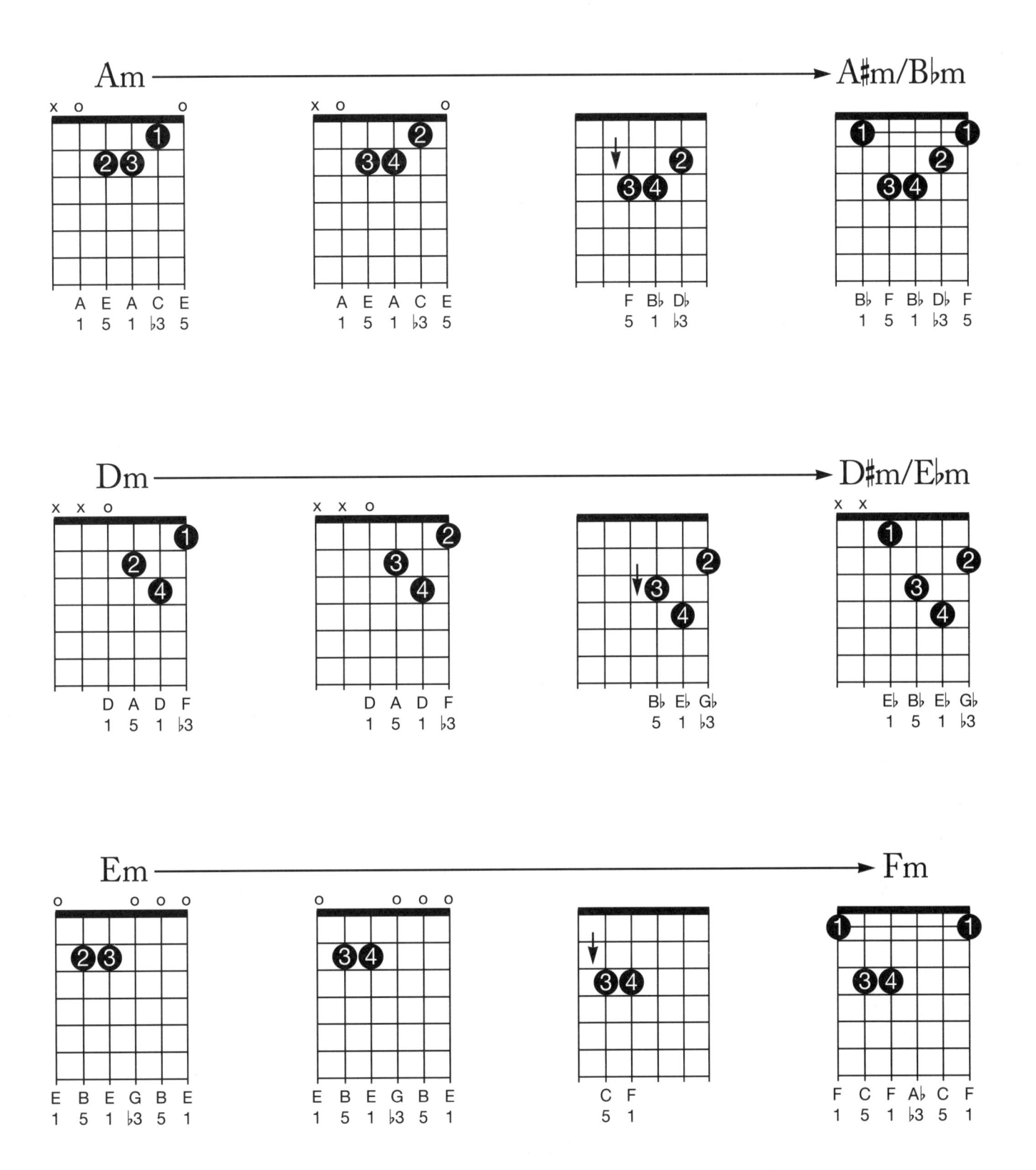

A E A C E	A E A C E	F B♭ D♭	B♭ F B♭ D♭ F
1 5 1 ♭3 5	1 5 1 ♭3 5	5 1 ♭3	1 5 1 ♭3 5

Dm → D#m/E♭m

D A D F	D A D F	B♭ E♭ G♭	E♭ B♭ E♭ G♭
1 5 1 ♭3	1 5 1 ♭3	5 1 ♭3	1 5 1 ♭3

Em → Fm

E B E G B E	E B E G B E	C F	F C F A♭ C F
1 5 1 ♭3 5 1	1 5 1 ♭3 5 1	5 1	1 5 1 ♭3 5 1

If you know how to use all these seven shapes you will have no less than 84 chords (7 shapes at 12 different frets) at your disposal!

35

▶▶ **PETE TOWNSHEND**
*"I suppose that I do sometimes sit down with an acoustic guitar
and try to use the guitar as an instrument of love and communication.
But even the way I play acoustic is very aggressively rhythmic."*

EASY   **INTERMEDIATE**   **ADVANCED**

9. Playing The Same Chord In Different Positions

The different, movable shapes you have just learnt enable you to play a major chord in four different places (the A, C, D and E shapes) and a minor chord in three places (the Am, Dm and Em shapes).

The chord boxes below show four A chords and three Am chords – each has its own distinctive sound. You could do the same thing with any other chord.

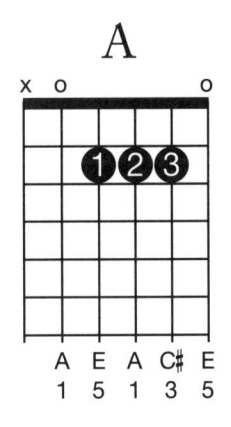

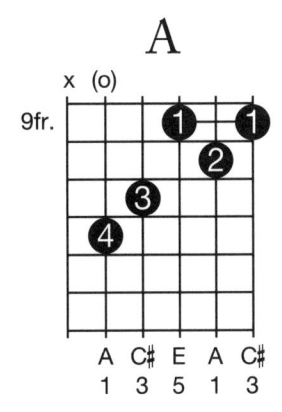

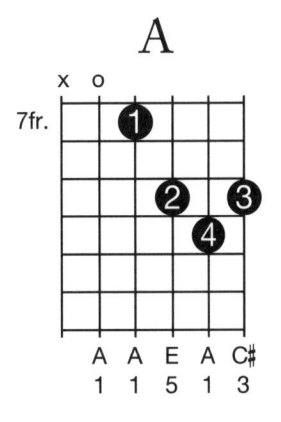

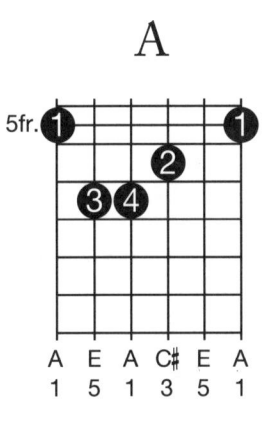

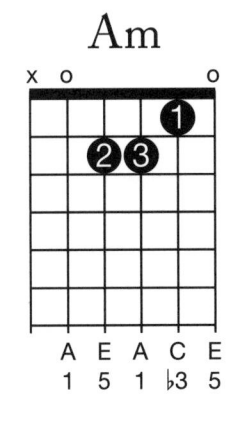

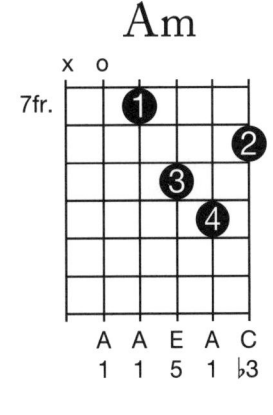

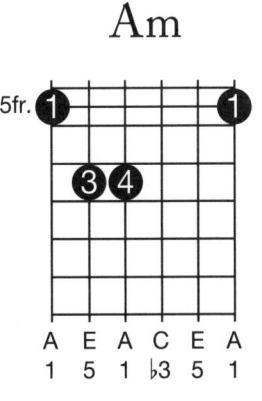

A
x o   o
A E A C# E
1 5 1 3 5

A
x (o)
9fr.
A C# E A C#
1 3 5 1 3

A
x o
7fr.
A A E A C#
1 1 5 1 3

A
5fr.
A E A C# E A
1 5 1 3 5 1

Am
x o   o
A E A C E
1 5 1 ♭3 5

Am
x o
7fr.
A A E A C
1 1 5 1 ♭3

Am
5fr.
A E A C E A
1 5 1 ♭3 5 1

Now you can go beyond major and minor and learn other types of chord.

37

Taking Chords Further
10. Woke Up This Mornin' – The Dominant Seventh

The next most popular group of chords after majors and minors are the dominant 7ths. This is a major chord with an extra note added one tone below the root note (the root note is the note after which a chord is named). So A7 is an A chord (A C♯ E) with a G added to it.

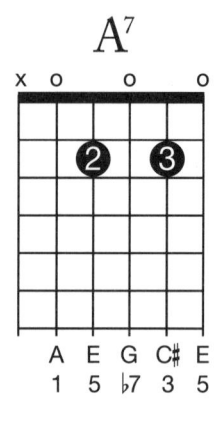

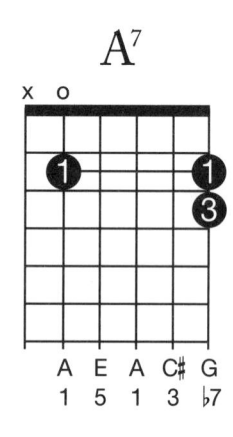

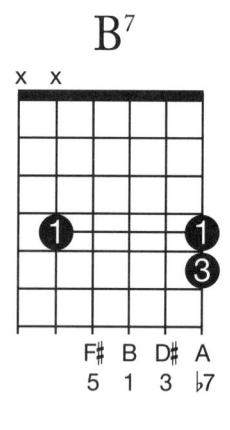

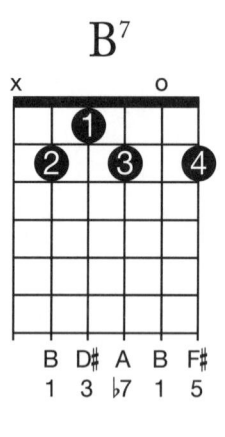

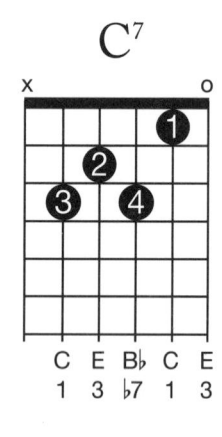

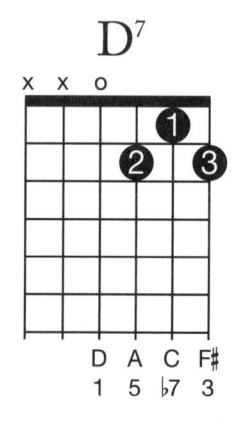

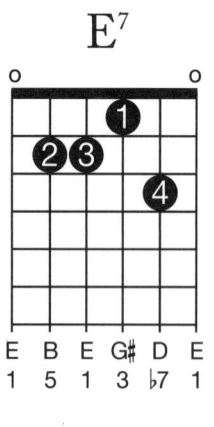

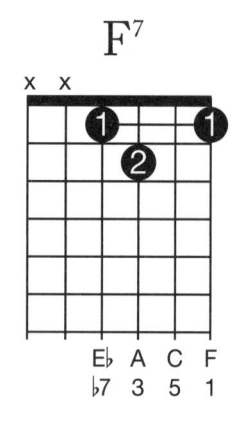

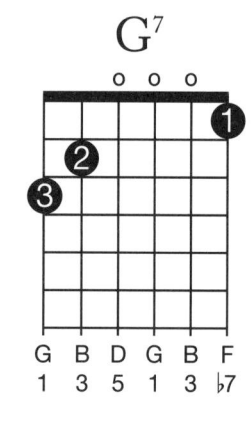

A⁷
x o o o
A E G C♯ E
1 5 ♭7 3 5

A⁷
x o
A E A C♯ G
1 5 1 3 ♭7

B⁷
x x
F♯ B D♯ A
5 1 3 ♭7

B⁷
x o
B D♯ A B F♯
1 3 ♭7 1 5

C⁷
x o
C E B♭ C E
1 3 ♭7 1 3

D⁷
x x o
D A C F♯
1 5 ♭7 3

E⁷
o o
E B E G♯ D E
1 5 1 3 ♭7 1

F⁷
x x
E♭ A C F
♭7 3 5 1

G⁷
o o o
G B D G B F
1 3 5 1 3 ♭7

These chords have a rough, bluesy sound, so it's no surprise that they're essential to acoustic and electric blues. You'll notice that there are two different shapes given above for A7 and B7 – they have the same notes, but in a slightly different arrangement. You can check this for yourself by referring to the letter names given at the bottom of the boxes. Where the extra note (the 'seventh') is played on the top string (as in boxes two and three) the chord has a 'spikier' sound.

Exercise 19

The 12-bar blues is a classic sequence used in thousands of blues and rock songs – here's your chance to have a go at a 12-bar progression in A.

Notice how the A7 in bar 4 leads the music to the D chord in the next bar, and how the D7 in bar 6 leads it back to A.

TRACKS 38+39

A			A⁷
4/4 / / / /	/ / / /	/ / / /	/ / / /

D	D⁷	A	A⁷
/ / / /	/ / / /	/ / / /	/ / / /

E E⁷	D⁷	A A⁷	E E⁷
/ / / /	/ / / /	/ / / /	/ / / /	

▶▶ JIMI HENDRIX
"You have to stick with it. Sometimes you are going to be so frustrated you want to give up the guitar. You'll hate the guitar. But all of this is just a part of learning because if you stick with it, you're going to be rewarded."

Exercise 20

Here's another 12-bar, this time in E. Every chord is now a dominant 7th, increasing the bluesy feel.

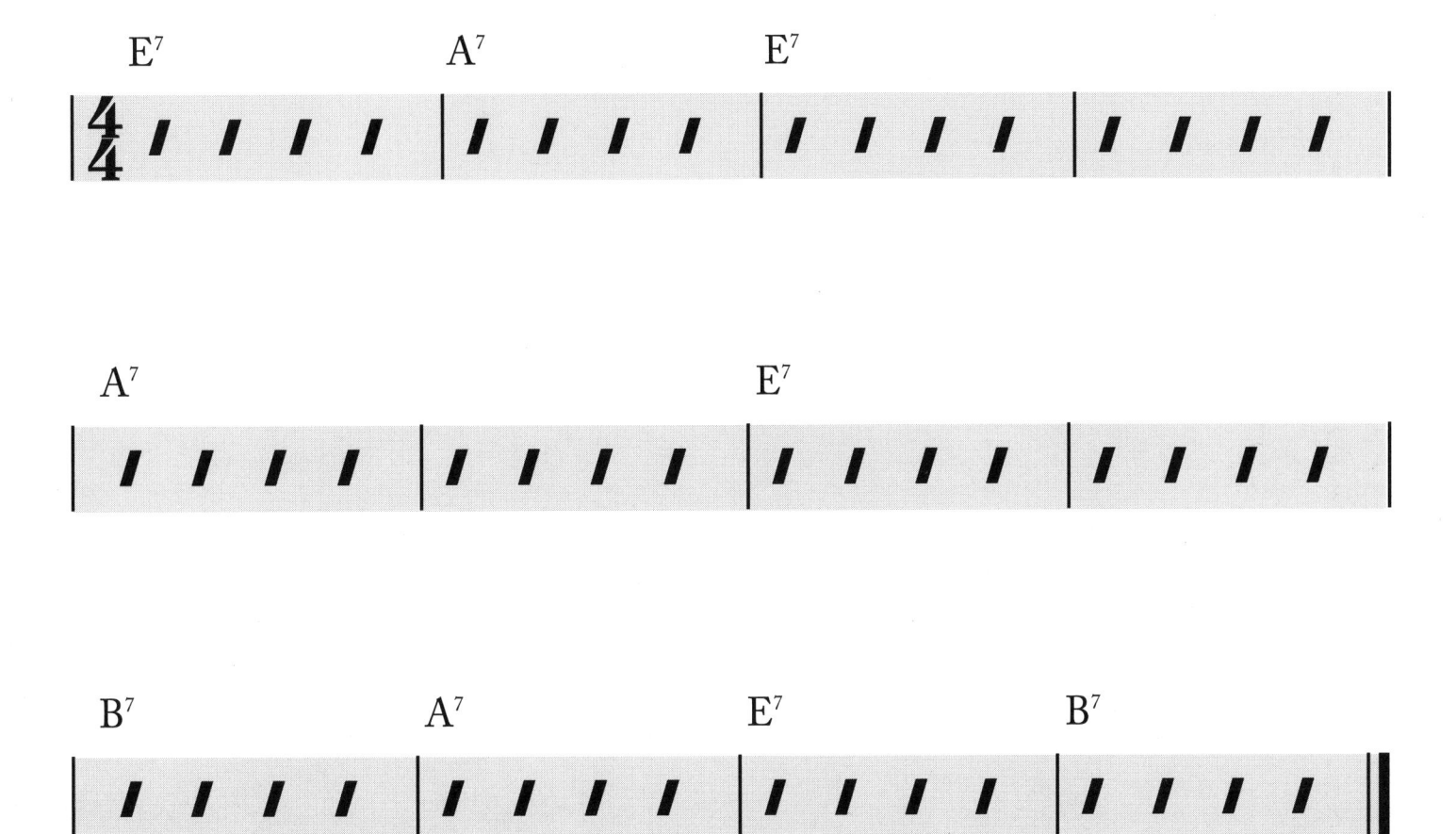

TRACKS 40+41

E^7	A^7	E^7	
4/4 / / / /	/ / / /	/ / / /	/ / / /

A^7		E^7	
/ / / /	/ / / /	/ / / /	/ / / /

B^7	A^7	E^7	B^7
/ / / /	/ / / /	/ / / /	/ / / /	

▶▶ **BRIAN MAY**
"Basically, I'm a real rock guitarist, but the term 'rock' is really wide these days. I like nearly everything that sounds honest and has some kind of statement."

Exercise 21

Note that when changing from C7 to D7 the
1st finger doesn't move.

TRACKS 42+43

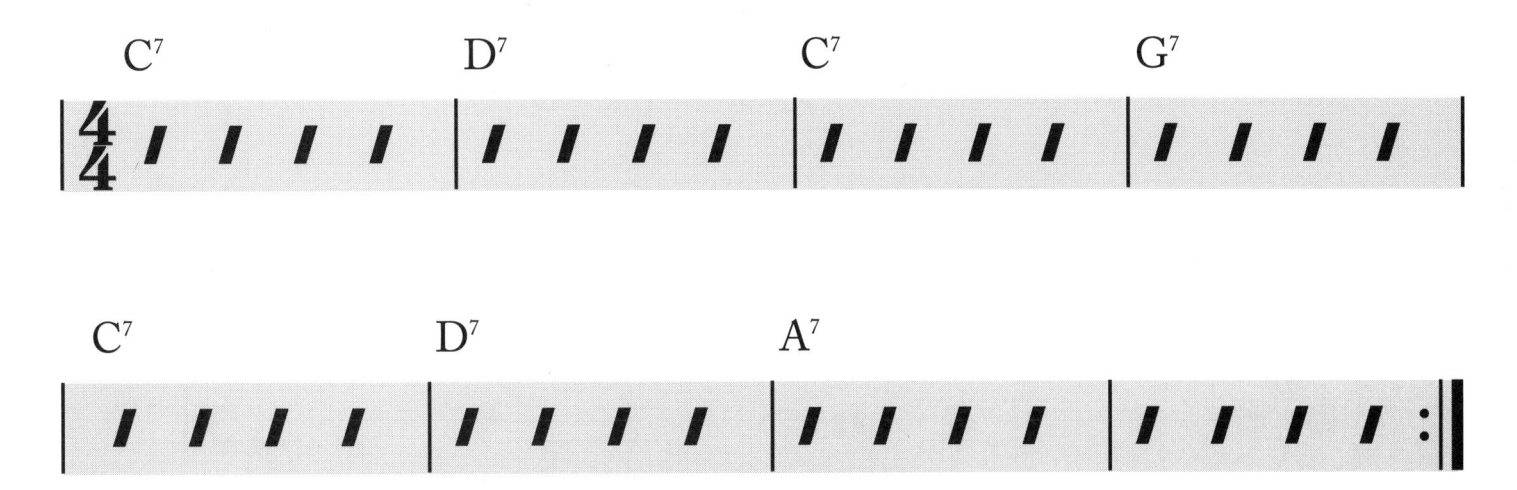

C7	D7	C7	G7
4/4 / / / /	/ / / /	/ / / /	/ / / /

C7	D7	A7	
/ / / /	/ / / /	/ / / /	/ / / / :||

Exercise 22

For the A7 in bar 2 use the first A7 box
until you can do the change easily – then try
substituting the alternative shape.

TRACKS 44+45

G7	A7	C7	D7
4/4 / / / /	/ / / /	/ / / /	/ / / / :||

11. This Chord's In Love – The Major Seventh

The major 7th is another major chord, but this time is has an extra note added a *semitone* below the root note. So Amaj7 is an A chord (A C♯ E) with a G♯ added. To avoid confusion with the dominant 7th chord, this one is written Amaj7.

These chords are romantic, and are particularly noticeable in the songs of writers like Burt Bacharach, or in the ballads of Lennon & McCartney. They are less common in rock and blues, but very popular in soul. In fact, the heavier rock gets the less likely you are to find a major 7th.

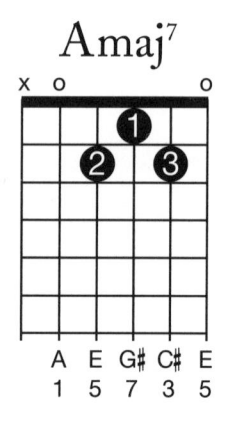

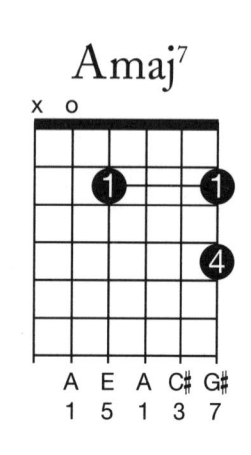

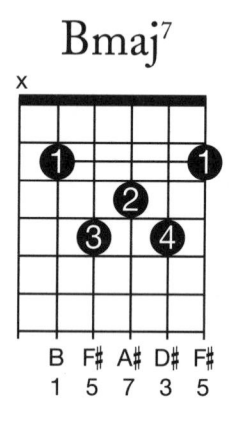

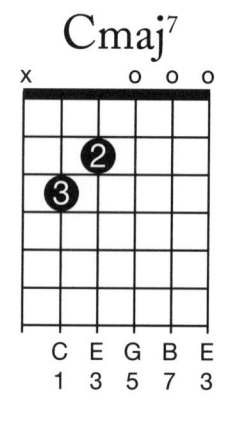

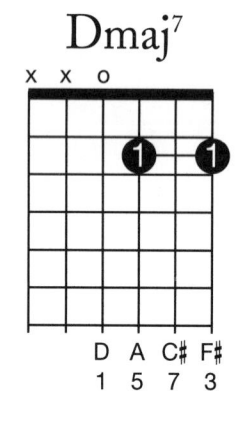

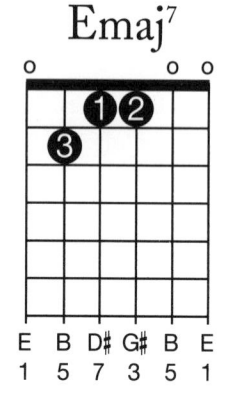

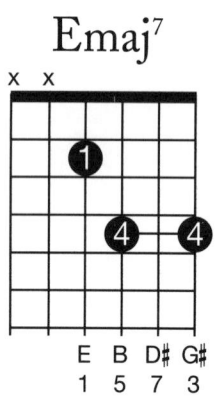

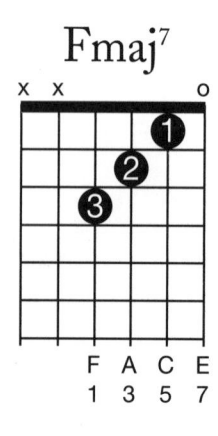

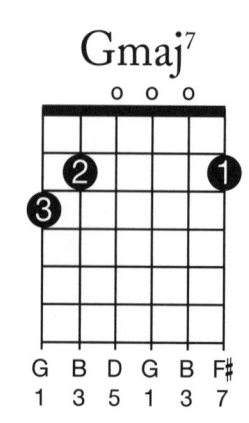

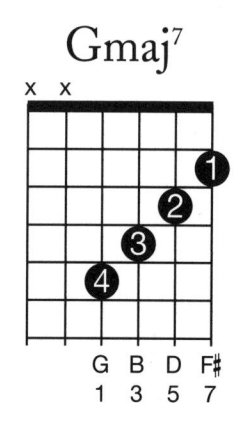

Amaj7
x o o
A E G♯ C♯ E
1 5 7 3 5

Amaj7
x o
A E A C♯ G♯
1 5 1 3 7

Bmaj7
x
B F♯ A♯ D♯ F♯
1 5 7 3 5

Cmaj7
x o o o
C E G B E
1 3 5 7 3

Dmaj7
x x o
D A C♯ F♯
1 5 7 3

Emaj7
o o o
E B D♯ G♯ B E
1 5 7 3 5 1

Emaj7
x x
E B D♯ G♯
1 5 7 3

Fmaj7
x x o
F A C E
1 3 5 7

Gmaj7
o o o
G B D G B F♯
1 3 5 1 3 7

Gmaj7
x x
G B D F♯
1 3 5 7

Exercise 23

This is a simple but summery change.

TRACKS 46+47

Amaj7		Dmaj7	
4/4 / / / /	/ / / /	/ / / /	/ / / / :||

Exercise 24

You are already familiar with Cmaj7, because it was one of the first 12 easy chords at the start of this book. When playing Gmaj7 it is possible to put the 2nd finger where the 3rd is on the bottom string – the 2nd finger then leans slightly to touch the 5th string, deadening it.

TRACKS 48+49

Cmaj7	Fmaj7	Cmaj7	Fmaj7
4/4 / / / /	/ / / /	/ / / /	/ / / /

Dmaj7	Gmaj7	Cmaj7	Gmaj7
/ / / /	/ / / /	/ / / /	/ / / / :||

JOHNNY MARR
"I listen for the things between chord changes, the thing that you almost play accidentally moving from one chord to another, and I try to fill those gaps. I try to glue together those harmonic and melodic overtones, and state the things that you imagine you're hearing."

Exercise 25

This example allows you to compare the dominant B7 with the different sound of the Amaj7 and Cmaj7.

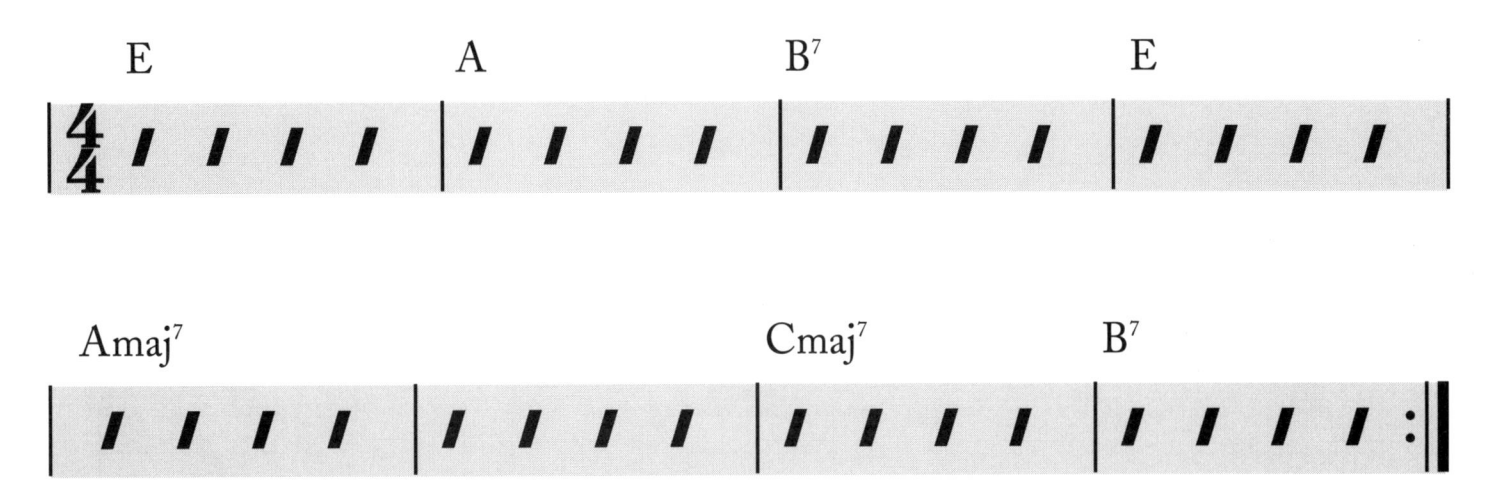

TRACKS 50+51

| E | A | B7 | E |
| Amaj7 | | Cmaj7 | B7 |

Exercise 26

In many songs, you will find a major chord changing to its major 7th, as is demonstrated here.

TRACKS 52+53

| C | Cmaj7 | Am | G |
| Fmaj7 | Em | Fmaj7 | G |

12. It's Getting Better – The Minor Seventh

The minor seventh is a minor chord with an extra note added a tone below the root note. So Am7 is an Am chord (A C E) with a G added.

These chords have a soft quality to them which makes them perfect for gentler music (combined with major 7th chords they often occur in soul music). They are much less common in rock and blues, although Thin Lizzy slipped a few minor 7ths into their hit *The Boys Are Back In Town*. Minor sevenths are not as sad, or as dark in mood as straight minor chords.

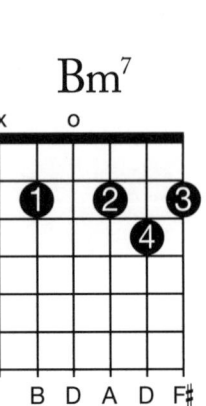

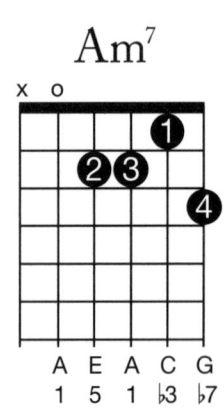

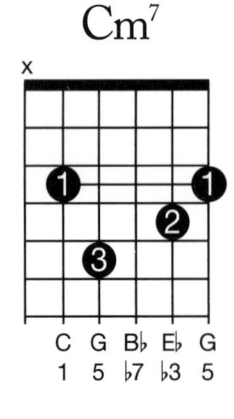

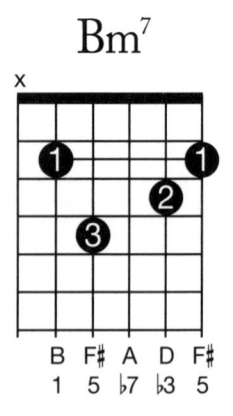

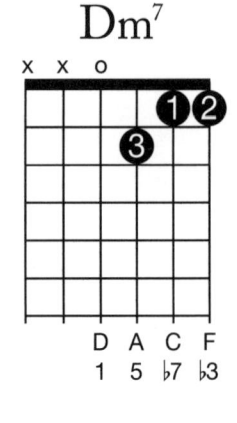

Am⁷
A E G C E
1 5 ♭7 ♭3 5

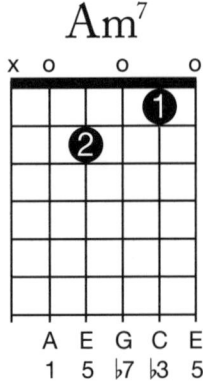

Am⁷
A E A C G
1 5 1 ♭3 ♭7

Bm⁷
B F♯ A D F♯
1 5 ♭7 ♭3 5

Bm⁷
B D A D F♯
1 ♭3 ♭7 ♭3 5

Cm⁷
C G B♭ E♭ G
1 5 ♭7 ♭3 5

Dm⁷
D A C F
1 5 ♭7 ♭3

Em⁷
E B E G D E
1 5 1 ♭3 ♭7 1

Fm⁷
E♭ A♭ C F
♭7 ♭3 5 1

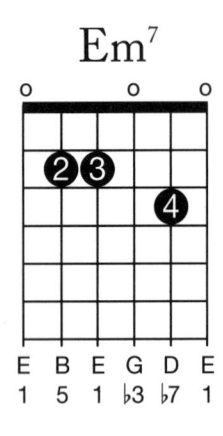

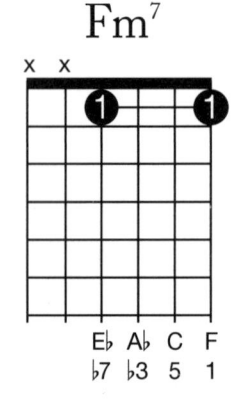

Gm⁷
G D F B♭ D G
1 5 ♭7 ♭3 5 1
(F)
(♭7)

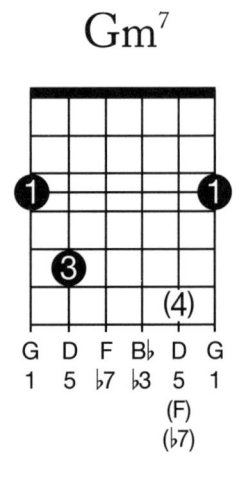

Exercise 27

This is a 12-bar blues in a minor key. To start with, try playing it with simple minor chords, and then add the minor 7ths – you'll hear the mood of the music brighten up.

TRACKS 54+55

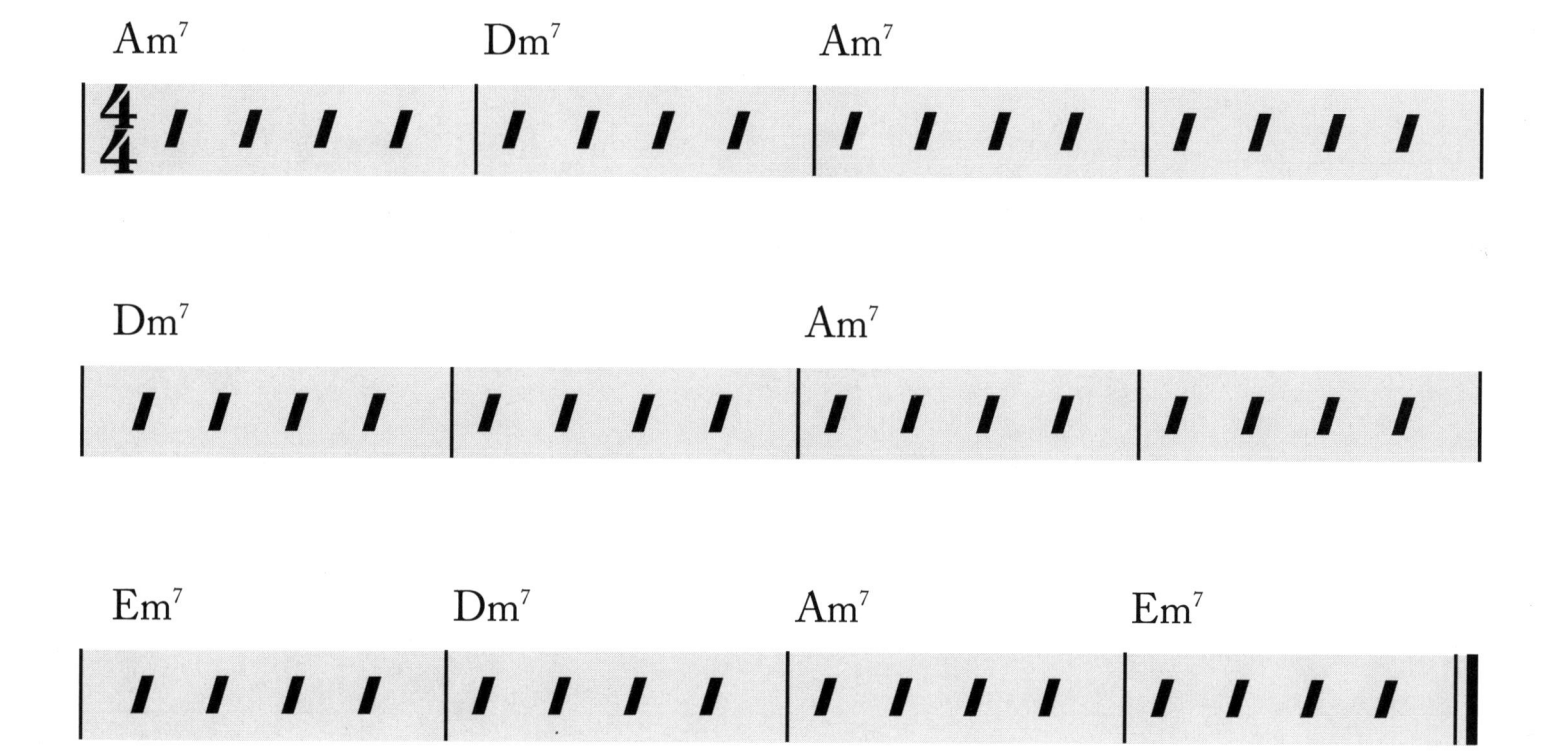

Am⁷	Dm⁷	Am⁷	
Dm⁷		Am⁷	
Em⁷	Dm⁷	Am⁷	Em⁷

Exercise 28

Here's a progression using the less common open string Bm7.

TRACKS 56+57

| Bm⁷ | Am⁷ | Em⁷ | Dm⁷ |

▶▶ *RY COODER*
"As a musician you should always have your ears open to other people's playing.
I'm always looking for a type of music that seems to be talking directly to me."

13. A Jagged Edge – The Suspended Fourth

The suspended 4th chord has real drama about it; it is formed when the note that tells you whether a chord is major or minor goes missing.

Here's how it works: the notes of an A *major* chord are A, C♯, and E, and the notes of an A *minor* chord are A, C, and E. The only note that distinguishes between them is the one in the middle (known as the 'third') – in an A major chord it is a C♯, but in an A minor chord it is a C. In a suspended 4th, that middle note rises to D. It sounds tense because it wants to fall back (resolve) either to C♯ or C. Suspended 4th chords are very common in pop, rock and folk – you will often hear them in the build-up toward the transition from one section of a song to another. For a concentrated dose of suspended 4ths try The Who's *Pinball Wizard*.

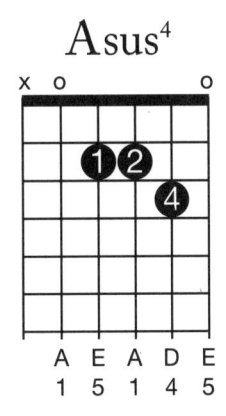

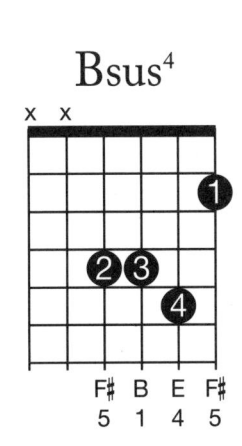

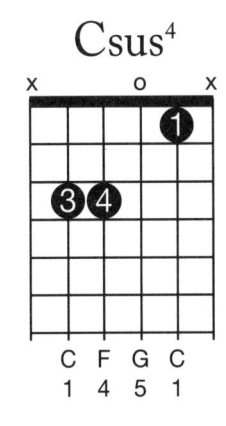

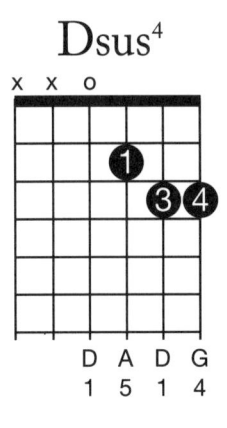

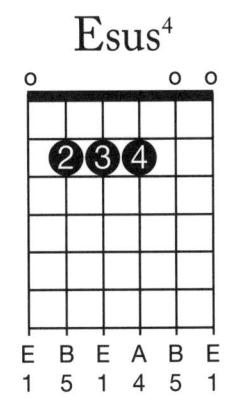

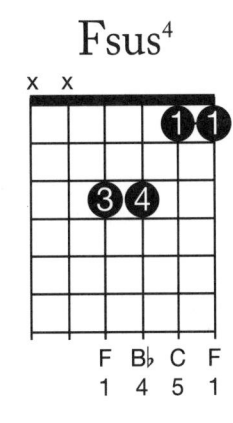

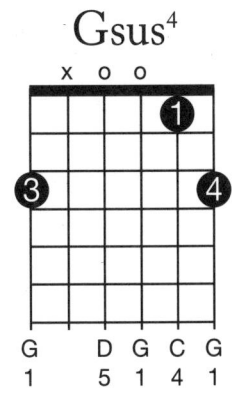

Asus⁴
A E A D E
1 5 1 4 5

Bsus⁴
F♯ B E F♯
5 1 4 5

Csus⁴
C F G C
1 4 5 1

Dsus⁴
D A D G
1 5 1 4

Esus⁴
E B E A B E
1 5 1 4 5 1

Fsus⁴
F B♭ C F
1 4 5 1

Gsus⁴
G D G C G
1 5 1 4 1

Exercise 29

For the change from F to Dm7 just lift your 3rd finger from the D string. Notice that in changing from Cmaj7 to F the 3rd finger doesn't move.

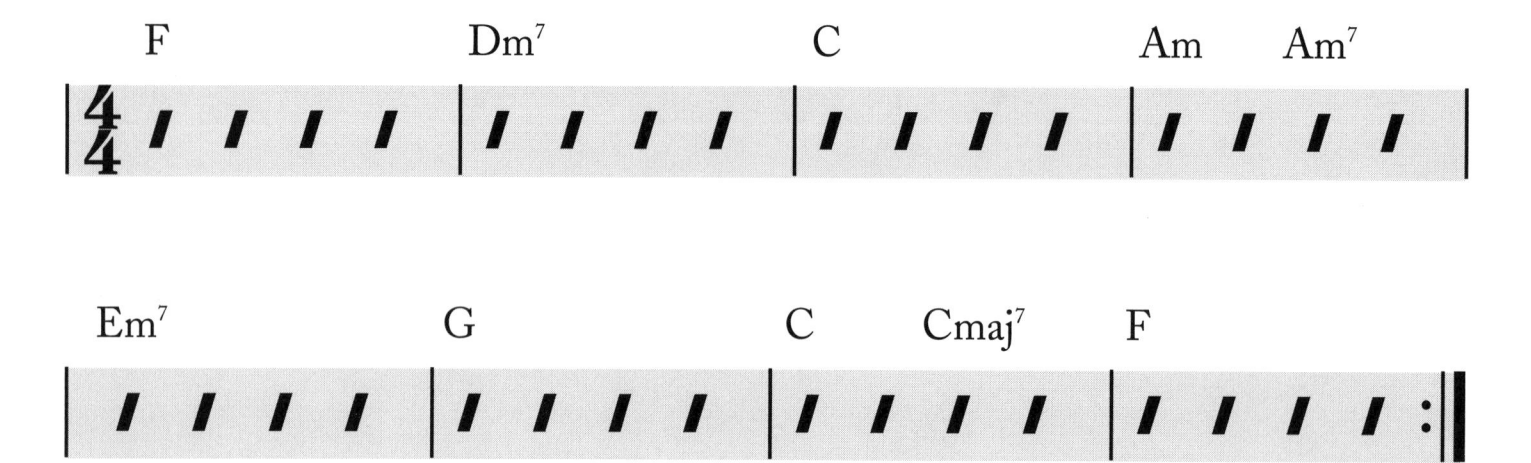

TRACKS 58+59

F	Dm⁷	C	Am　Am⁷
4/4 / / / /	/ / / /	/ / / /	/ / / /

Em⁷	G	C　Cmaj⁷	F
/ / / /	/ / / /	/ / / /	/ / / / :||

Exercise 30

For the Fm7, either use the half barre version shown above, or take the Gm7 shape and move it down to the first fret.

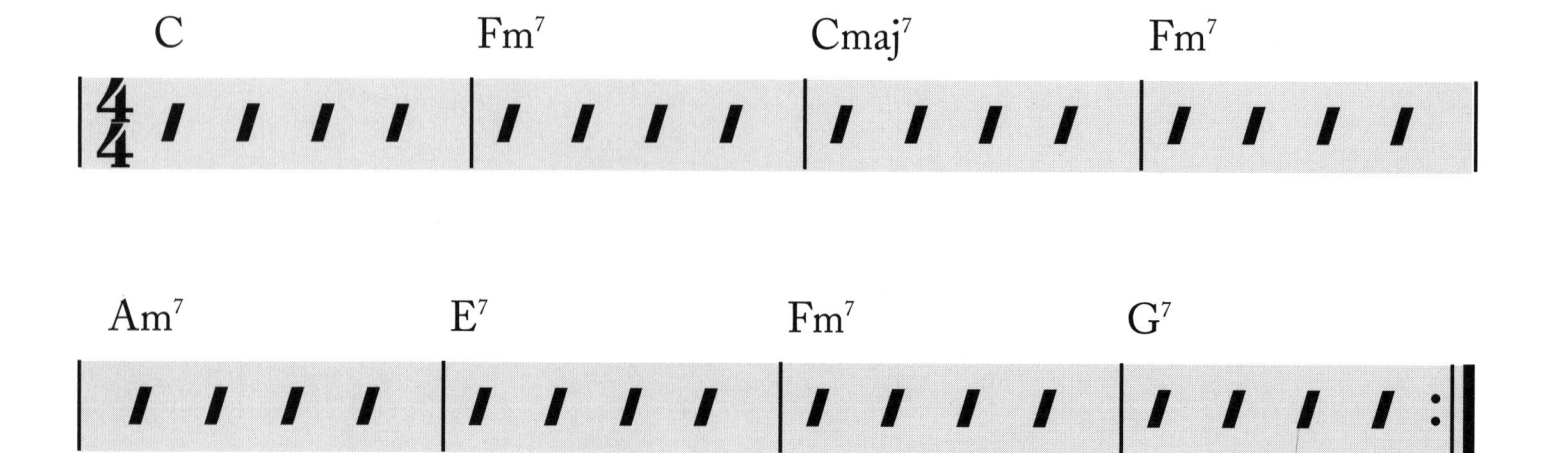

TRACKS 60+61

C	Fm⁷	Cmaj⁷	Fm⁷
4/4 / / / /	/ / / /	/ / / /	/ / / /

Am⁷	E⁷	Fm⁷	G⁷
/ / / /	/ / / /	/ / / /	/ / / / :||

52　▶▶FastForward Acoustic Guitar Chords

Exercise 31

Here are two of the most popular suspended 4th changes.

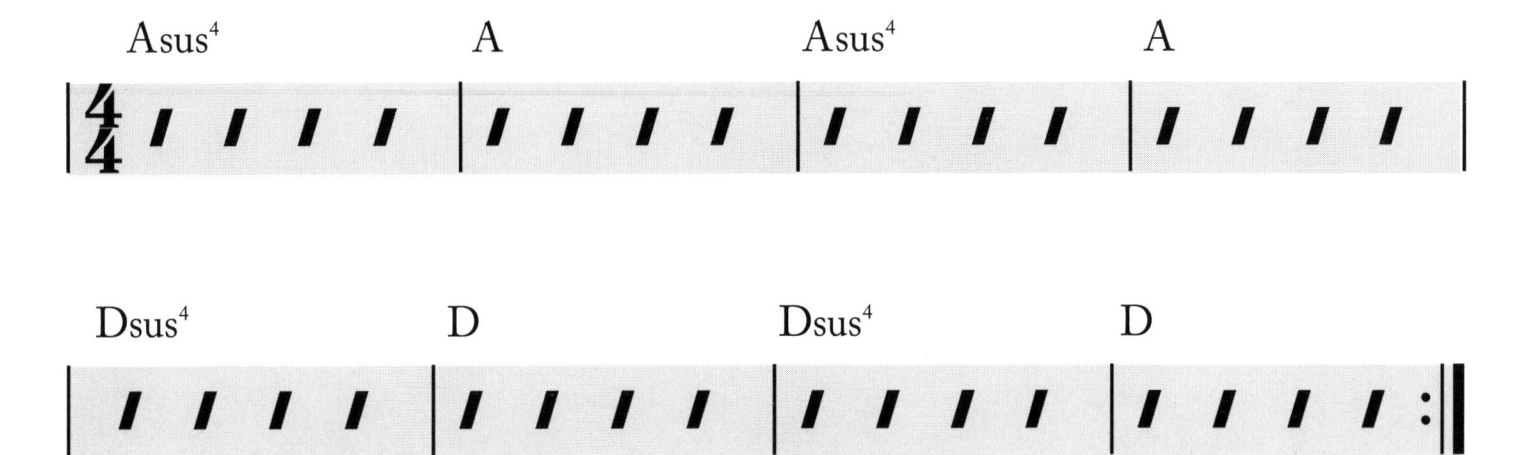

TRACKS 62+63

Asus⁴	A	Asus⁴	A
4/4 / / / /	/ / / /	/ / / /	/ / / /

Dsus⁴	D	Dsus⁴	D
/ / / /	/ / / /	/ / / /	/ / / / :||

Exercise 32

Notice that when you change from G to Dsus4 the little finger on the top string doesn't move.

TRACKS 64+65

Gsus⁴	G	Dsus⁴	D
4/4 / / / /	/ / / /	/ / / /	/ / / /

Esus⁴	E	Asus⁴	A
/ / / /	/ / / /	/ / / /	/ / / / :||

14. Tension On The Highwire – The Suspended Second

The suspended 2nd chord is not quite as dramatic as the suspended 4th, although it can have an empty, spacy sound. It is also formed when the note that tells you whether a chord is major or minor goes missing.

Here the third of the chord falls to the second note of the scale. So A (A C# E) becomes Asus2 (A B E). It sounds tense because the B wants to rise to C or C#.

Suspended 2nds are common in pop, rock and folk, often combined with suspended 4ths. For a classic example listen to John Lennon's *Happy Xmas (War Is Over)*.

Asus²
A E A B E
1 5 1 2 5

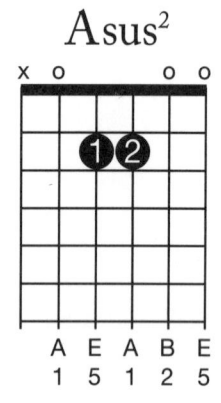

Bsus²
B F# B C# F#
1 5 1 2 5

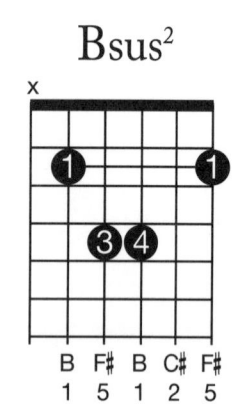

Csus²
C D G C
1 2 5 1

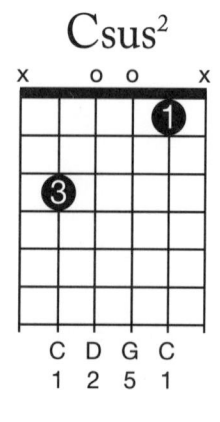

Csus²
C G C D G
1 5 1 2 5

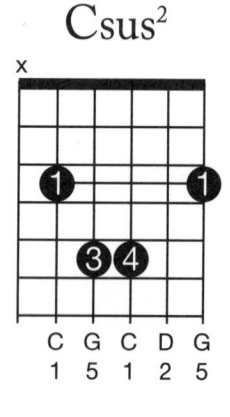

Dsus²
D A D E
1 5 1 2

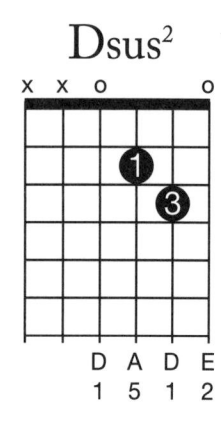

Esus²
E B F# B B E
1 5 2 5 5 1

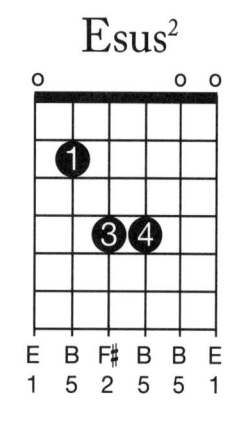

Fsus²
F G C F
1 2 5 1

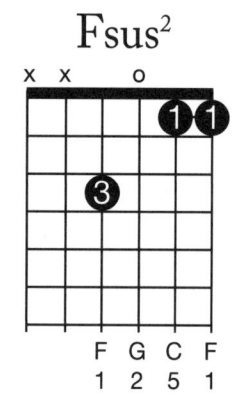

Gsus²
G D A D G
1 5 2 5 1

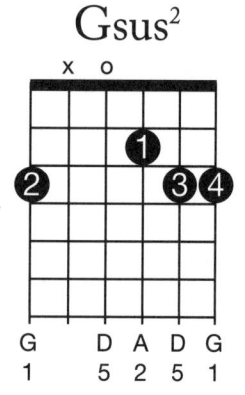

Exercise 33

The Asus2 and Dsus2 chords are popular because you only have to lift a finger off!

TRACKS 66+67

A	Asus²	D	Dsus²
4/4 / / / /	/ / / /	/ / / /	/ / / /

Esus²		Asus²	A
/ / / /	/ / / /	/ / / /	/ / / / :||

Exercise 34

The sound of a suspended 2nd chord changes depending on how low or high in the chord the 2nd is. If you look at the numbers below the chord shapes you can see that the first Csus2 shape has the 2 on the 4th string, while the Dsus2 has it on the top string. Compare their different sounds in this exercise.

TRACKS 68+69

Csus²	C	Fsus²	F
4/4 / / / /	/ / / /	/ / / /	/ / / /

Dsus²	Dm	Gsus²	G
/ / / /	/ / / /	/ / / /	/ / / / :||

Exercise 35

This sequence shows how the suspended 2nd can turn into either a minor or a major chord.

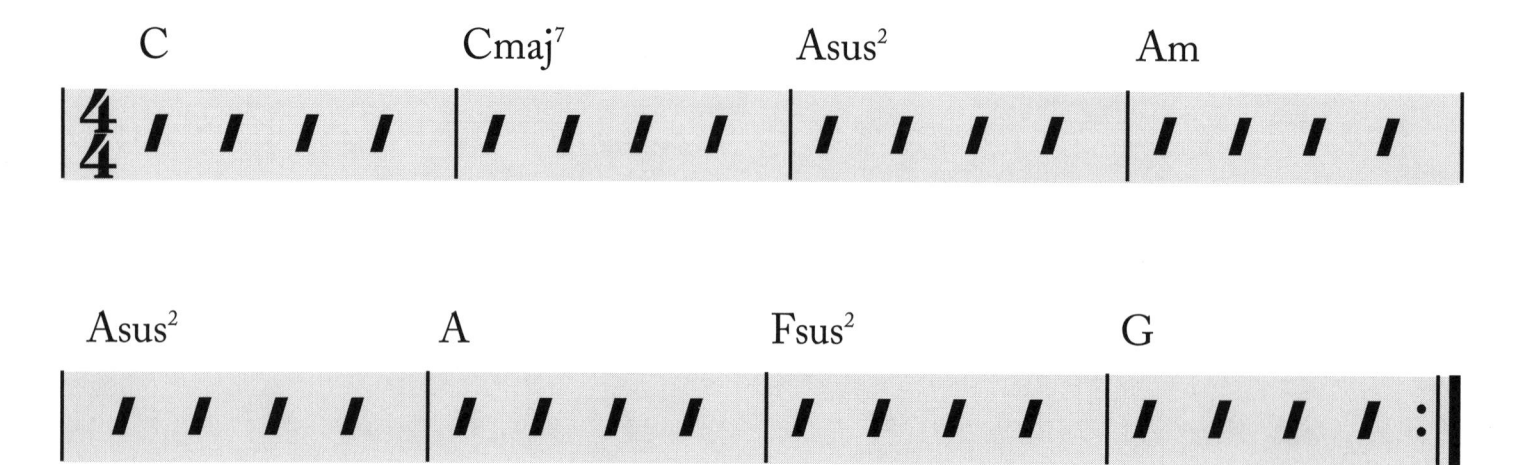

TRACKS 70+71

| C | Cmaj7 | Asus2 | Am |
| Asus2 | A | Fsus2 | G |

Exercise 36

Finally, here's a sequence that combines suspended 4ths and 2nds.

TRACKS 72+73

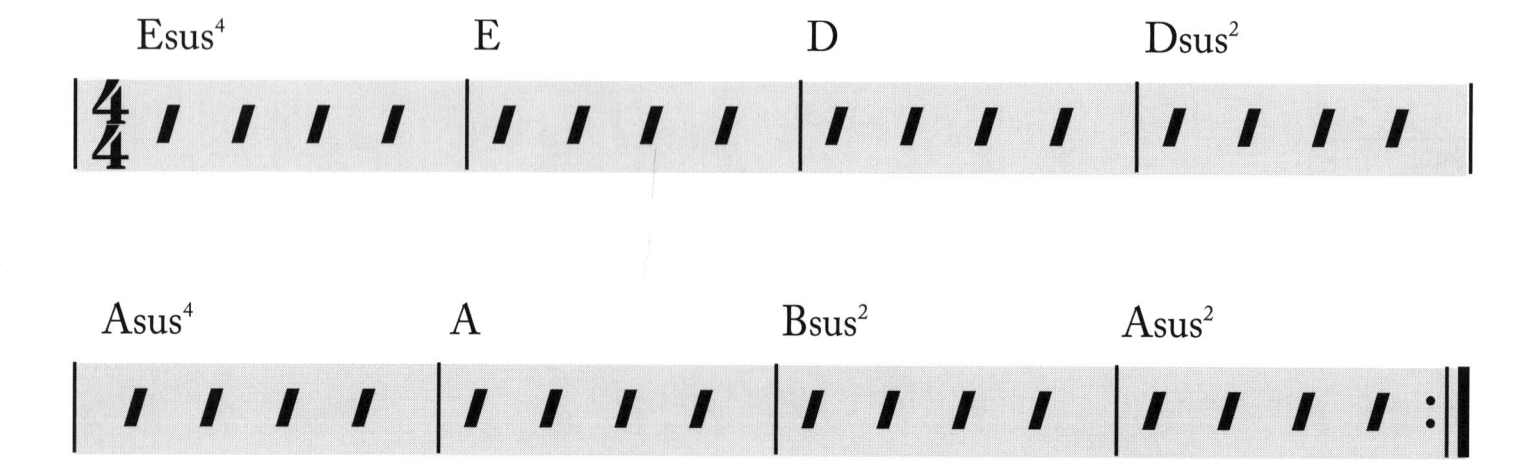

| Esus4 | E | D | Dsus2 |
| Asus4 | A | Bsus2 | Asus2 |

15. Just Fab – Major Sixths

The major 6th chord takes a major chord and adds the sixth note of the scale. The result is a slightly jazzy, colourful chord with a mild tension. The major 6th is closely related to the minor 7th:

    G6 = G B D E

    Em7 = E G B D

Same notes, different root!

A certain famous beat group from Liverpool in the 1960s were quite partial to the odd major 6th, either on the guitar or in the vocal harmonies. Listen to the last chord of *She Loves You* and compare it with the last chord of Roxy Music's *Love Is The Drug* – both are major 6ths.

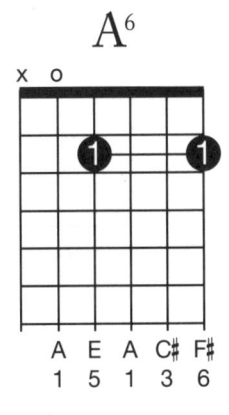

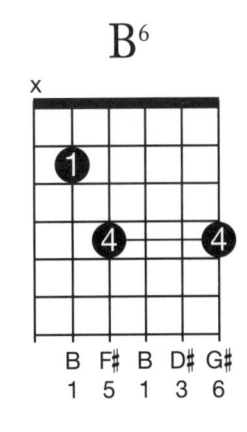

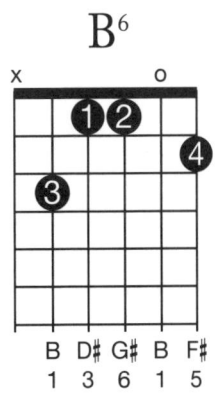

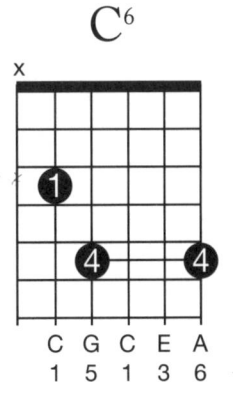

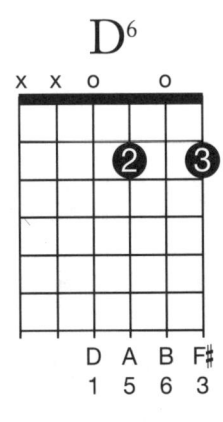

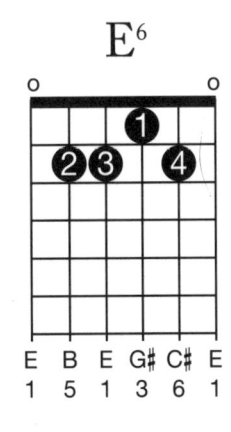

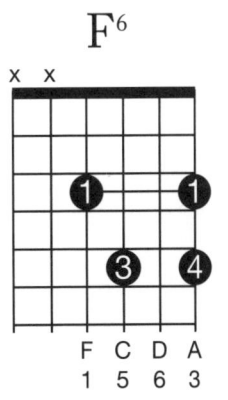

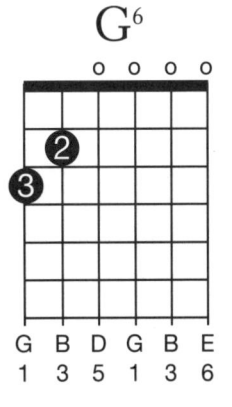

A^6
A E A C# F#
1 5 1 3 6

B^6
B F# B D# G#
1 5 1 3 6

B^6
B D# G# B F#
1 3 6 1 5

C^6
C G C E A
1 5 1 3 6

D^6
D A B F#
1 5 6 3

E^6
E B E G# C# E
1 5 1 3 6 1

F^6
F C D A
1 5 6 3

G^6
G B D G B E
1 3 5 1 3 6

Most of these chords are quite easy, as long as you're happy doing half-barres. The little finger barres in the B6 and C6 shapes may take a bit more time – you'll need to build up strength in your 4th finger.

Exercise 37

This progression can be played with one finger!

TRACKS 74+75

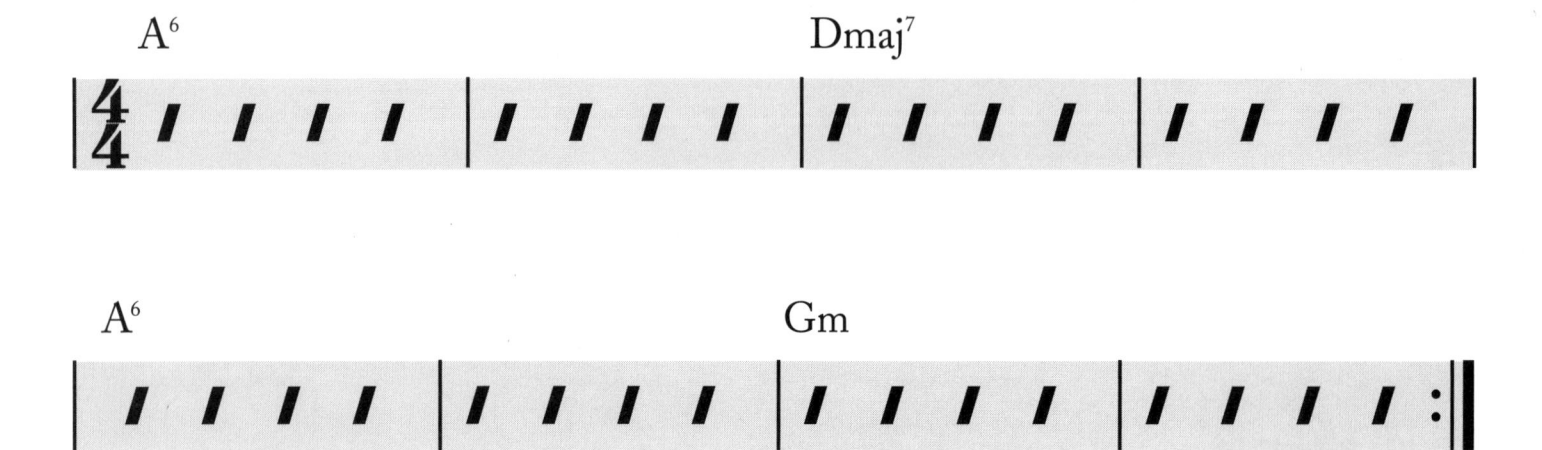

A⁶		Dmaj⁷	
/ / / /	/ / / /	/ / / /	/ / / /

A⁶		Gm	
/ / / /	/ / / /	/ / / /	/ / / / :||

Exercise 38

Watch out for the B6 here. If you can't manage the little finger barre just move the A6 chord up two frets – but make sure you don't hit the lower two strings!

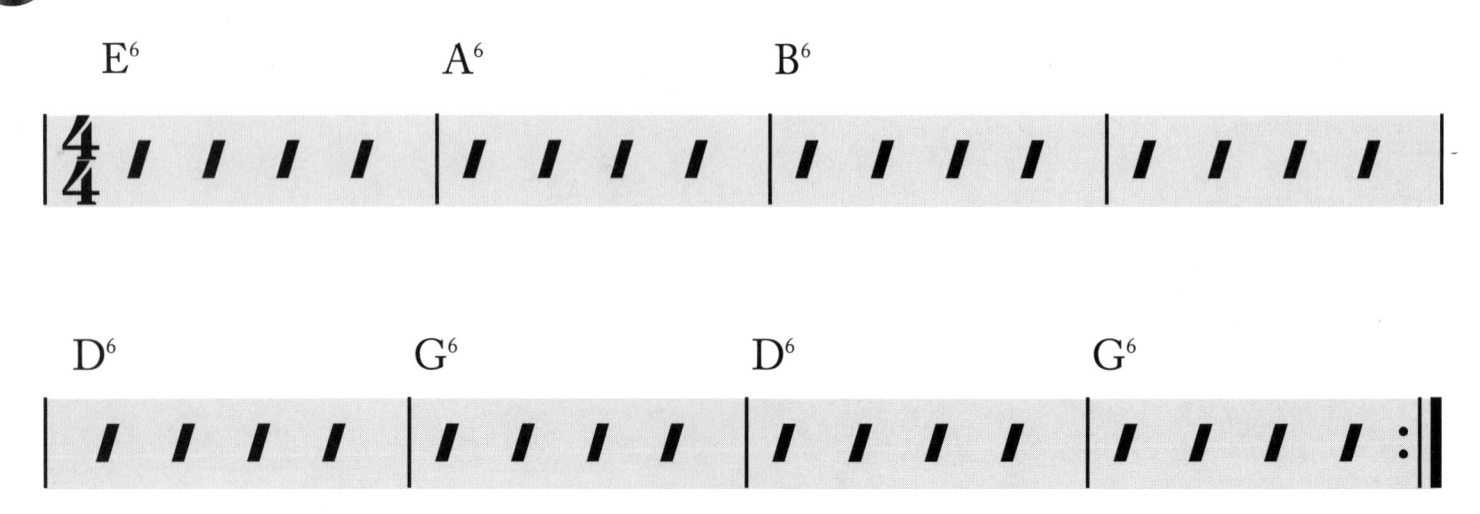

TRACKS 76+77

E⁶	A⁶	B⁶	
/ / / /	/ / / /	/ / / /	/ / / /

D⁶	G⁶	D⁶	G⁶
/ / / /	/ / / /	/ / / /	/ / / / :||

Exercise 39

This E-E6 change can have a rock 'n' roll effect.

TRACKS 78+79

| E E⁶ | E E⁶ | A⁶ | B⁶ :|

Exercise 40

This exercise mixes some major 6ths with other chords. Notice that the G6 and Em chords have a very similar sound!

TRACKS 80+81

| A⁶ | Bm | Gmaj⁷ | Dmaj⁷ |

| Em | G⁶ | Em | G⁶ :|

Putting It All Together
16. Complete Song – Tuesday's Queen

Now that you have mastered the full range of guitar chords, you're ready to try a full song of chord-changes. *Tuesday's Queen* has a typical pop song structure:

> Intro (4 bars)
> Verse (16 bars)
> Chorus (8 bars)
> Verse 2
> Chorus 2
> Middle 8 with Solo (8 bars)
> Chorus 3
> Chorus 4
> Coda (9 bars)

It's in the key of A and uses a variety of chords throughout. Watch out for the F♯m – to play this as a half-barre, refer to the Fm shape in section 3 and move it up one fret. To play the full barre version refer to the version of Fm given in section 8 and move that up one fret. Play steadily and smoothly.

TRACKS 82+83

Tuesday's Queen

Intro

A	Dmaj⁷ E	A	Dmaj⁷ E
4/4 / / / /	/ / / /	/ / / /	/ / / /	

Verse

A	A⁷	Bm	Dsus²
/ / / /	/ / / /	/ / / /	/ / / /

A	A⁷	Bm	E
/ / / /	/ / / /	/ / / /	/ / / /

Dsus⁴ D	Esus⁴ E	F♯m	
/ / / /	/ / / /	/ / / /	/ / / /

60 ▶▶ FastForward Acoustic Guitar Chords

| D / / / / | Dmaj⁷ / / / / | Bm / / / / | E / / / / ‖

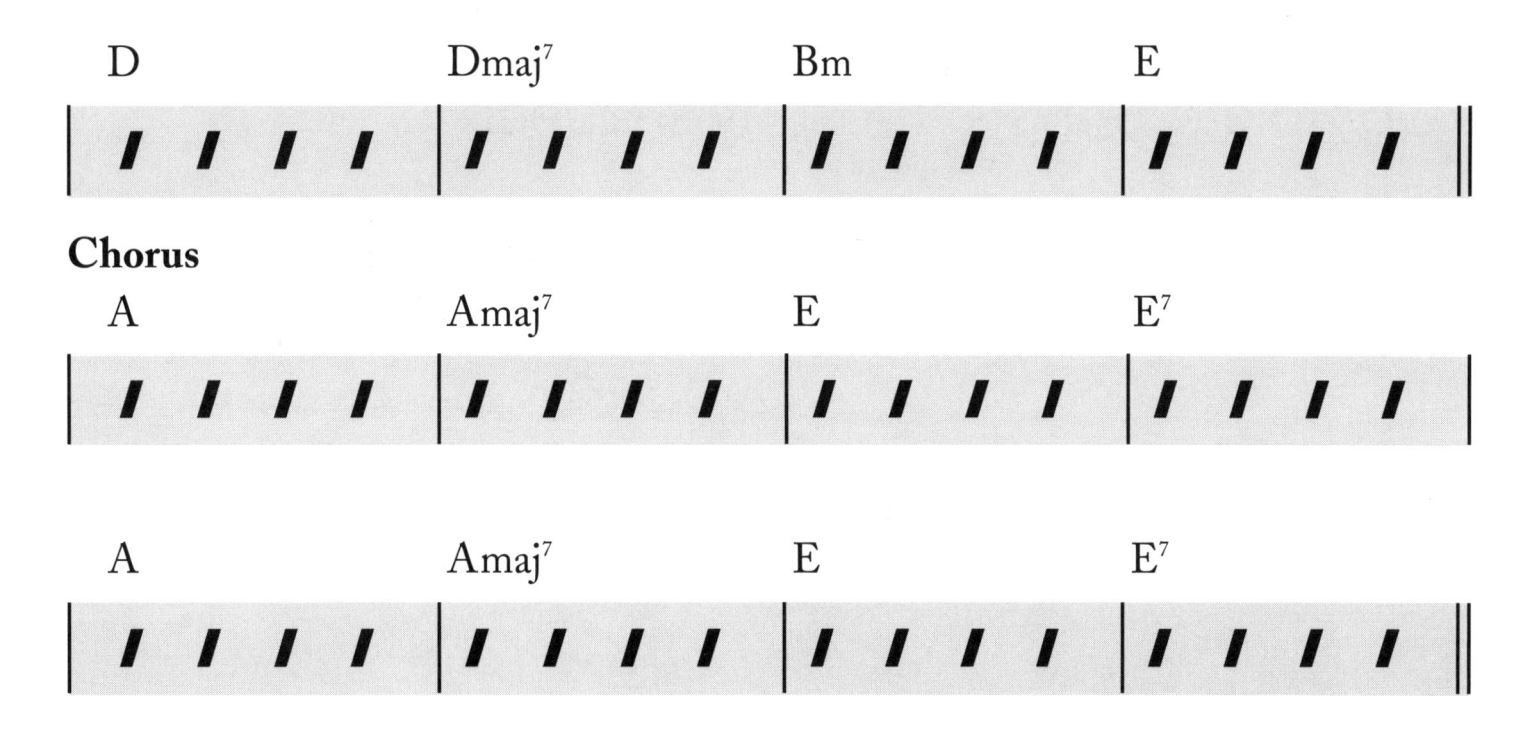

Chorus

| A / / / / | Amaj⁷ / / / / | E / / / / | E⁷ / / / / |

| A / / / / | Amaj⁷ / / / / | E / / / / | E⁷ / / / / ‖

Repeat Verse and Chorus

Middle Eight

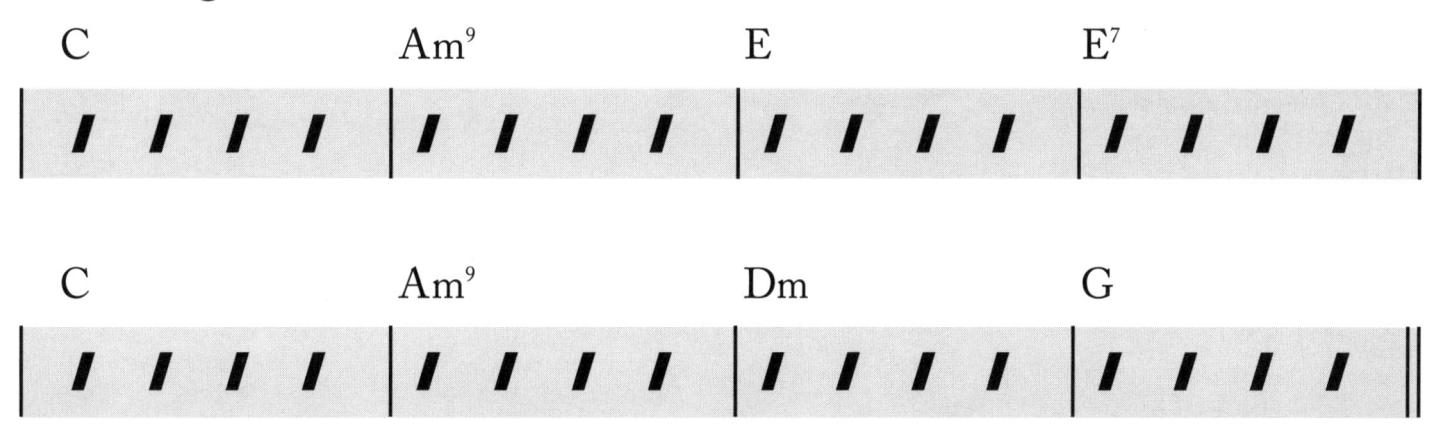

| C / / / / | Am⁹ / / / / | E / / / / | E⁷ / / / / |

| C / / / / | Am⁹ / / / / | Dm / / / / | G / / / / ‖

Repeat Chorus Twice

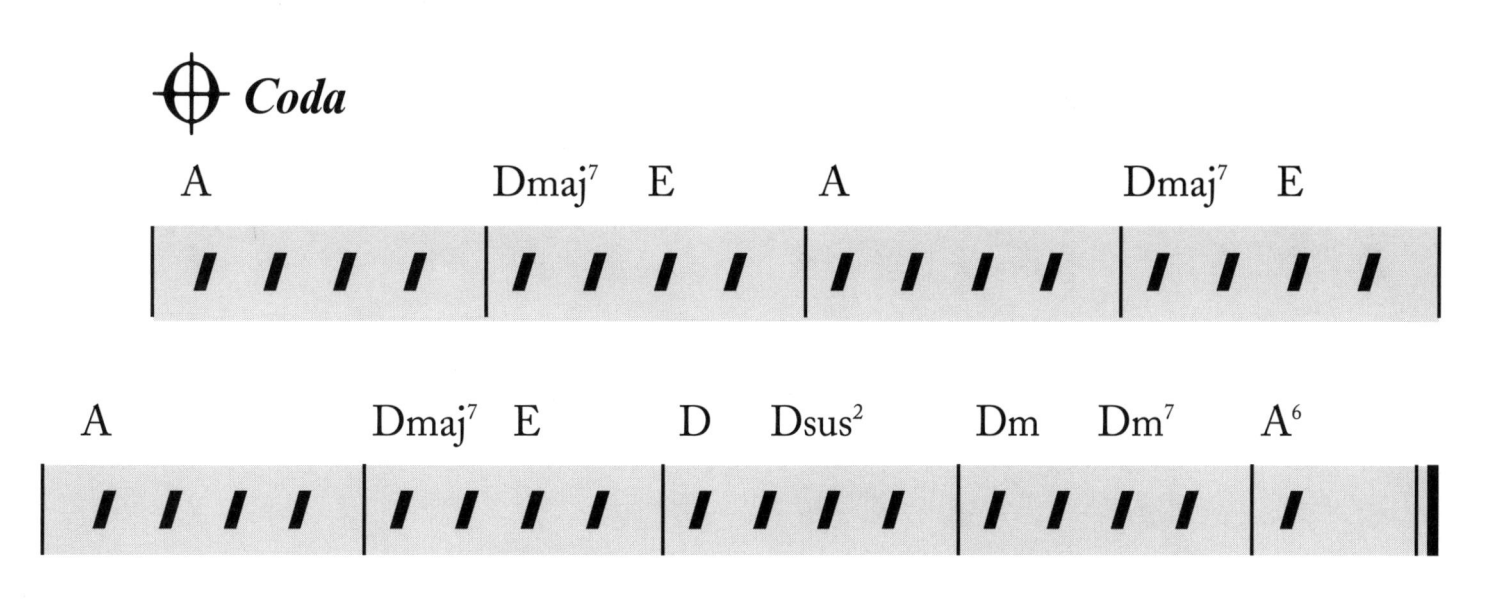

⊕ *Coda*

| A / / / / | Dmaj⁷ / / E / / | A / / / / | Dmaj⁷ / / E / / |

| A / / / / | Dmaj⁷ / / E / / | D / / Dsus² / / | Dm / Dm⁷ / A⁶ / ‖

▶▶ *MARC BOLAN*
"I have days where I'm just a guitarist and I play guitar all day and I just don't want to sing."

Congratulations!

If you've learned all the chords in this book and you can play them along with the backing tracks, you will be able to strum many popular songs. Explore some of the titles listed below and you will soon be strumming along with all your favourite songs. You may even be able to put some of these chords together and write some songs of your own!

The Complete Guitar Player Beatles Songbook
NO18491

The Complete Guitar Player Chord Book
AM939279 (Book + CD)

The Complete Guitar Player Chord Encyclopedia
AM90134 (Book + CD)

The Complete Guitar Player Eric Clapton
AM83593

The Complete Guitar Player Bob Dylan
AM79229

The Complete Guitar Player Paul Simon
PS10875

The Complete Guitar Player Songbook Omnibus
AM75797

Beatles Guitar
NO18798

Blur For Easy Guitar Tab
AM936859

Play Guitar With Blur
AM935320 (Book + CD)

Eric Clapton: Crossroads
AM92316 (3 volumes)

Jimi Hendrix: Radio One
AM91394

Official Guitar Styles Of Mark Knopfler
DG70636

Bob Marley: Songs Of Freedom
AM933504

Metallica: The Collection
AM92311 (4 volumes)

The Other Side Of Oasis
AM939037

Play Guitar With Oasis
AM935330 (Book + CD)

Oasis: (What's The Story) Morning Glory
AM934802

Play Guitar With Pulp
AM938124 (Book + CD)

Play Guitar With Rolling Stones
AM90247 (Book + CD)

Play Guitar With Paul Weller
AM937827 (Book + CD)

Play Guitar With Chuck Berry
AM943789 (Book + CD)

Beatles Chord Songbook
NO90664

Blur Chord Songbook
AM936914

Oasis Chord Songbook
AM936903

Alanis Morissette: Jagged Little Pill
AM937684

▶▶ **DAMON ALBARN**
"My songs are very uncoordinated and disparate ... just basic melodies and major or minor chords."